COMING THROUGH THE FIRE

COMING

THROUGH

THE FIRE

Surviving Race and

Place in America

C. ERIC LINCOLN

DUKE UNIVERSITY PRESS

Durham and London 1996

© 1996 Duke University Press

All rights reserved

Printed in the United States of

America on acid-free paper ∞

Typeset in Berkeley Medium by

Tseng Information Systems, Inc.

Library of Congress Cataloging-

in-Publication Data appear on the

last printed page of this book.

This book is dedicated to
R. EUGENE PINCHAM
MARY LOUISE WRIGHT

With grateful appreciation
to the Eli Lilly Foundation
for research support.

CONTENTS

I

NOTES ON RACE

America

My native land

How long this road since freedom.

—C. ERIC LINCOLN,

This Road since Freedom

Coming through the Fire began as "Notes on Race" in the series of journals I kept from 1941 until they were destroyed by fire fifty years later. I am not exactly certain of what I intended to do with the thousands of entries made under "Race," but I found the whole matter of racist behavior fascinating and spent many, many hours over the decades detached from my own involuntary participation in the phenomenon, trying to understand its logic and account for its pervasiveness.

Some of my "Notes on Race" found their way into other writings, such as my novel (*The Avenue, Clayton City*), my poetry (*This Road since Freedom*), and a book of essays called *Race, Religion, and the Continuing American Dilemma*. But the sheer volume and variety of my racial experience, personal and vicarious, would require the innocence of uninhibited imagination to accept as true. Such an innocence is hard to come by in this age of hypersophistication, even though my experiences are scarcely unique. In fact, they were routine and even normative in the settings in which they occurred. Many of the racial encounters I remember most vividly seem especially cruel for what they did to the children who were so generously misendowed with the legacies of hatred and denigration endemic to the culture.

Once, I was on a train going from Chicago to St. Louis when "Dinner in the diner!" was announced. I joined the line of passengers moving slowly into the dining car and found myself directly behind a well-dressed young matron with a child of five or six clinging possessively to her mother's skirts as she discovered me looming above her.

"Mommie," the little girl announced in a confidential stage whisper: "Mommie, there is a 'zigaboo' behind you!" The mother turned and looked squarely into my eyes. Did *she* see a "zigaboo?" I wondered. She gave no hint.

"Shut up!" the mommie said, turning a bit rosy, "just shut up!"

"But *Mom-mee*," the little tyke insisted, and this time with more exasperation than confidentiality, "Well there is so an old black you-know-what on this train, and he's standing . . . !"

"Penny, will you just please shut up?" the mother snapped above the cacophony of snickers that rippled down the dinner line. She then dragged the very frustrated and bewildered young child back into the lounge car. I worried that the little girl would miss her dinner because nobody had yet told her when to just *think* "zigaboo" (whatever that is!) without announcing it to all creation. You don't have to make announcements to people whose racial receptors have already made the determinations for themselves.

Some experiences are so bizarre as to defy all reason.

In the wake of the television presentation of Alex Haley's classic *Roots*, many Americans journeyed to Africa in search of their own ancestral moorings, while some others just went to see what the noise was all about. On one occasion I found myself in the airport at Accra, Ghana, whiling away the time until my plane would leave for New York. The airport was teeming with black faces as far as the eye could see: Ghanians, Nigerians, Ivoreans, Senegalese, Christians, Muslims, etc., in European dress or distinctive tribal costumes. Suddenly my eyes met those of a tall, bronzed, gray-haired Westerner sporting a ten-gallon Stetson hat, hand-decorated western boots, a string tie, and, as it turned out, a very sonorous Texas drawl. The "Texan" was the only "white" person in sight, and he was headed directly toward me. He strode over to where I was standing, pushed his Stetson back a bit, and stared down at me, his gray eyes twinkling with uninhibited pleasure as they squinted through the crow's-feet etched by a thousand Texas dust storms. Touching my arm with a gesture of camaraderie, he asked in a friendly, almost confidential voice: "You wouldn't be from the United States, would you, Pardner?" I confirmed that I was.

"Well, by Gawd, I-just-be-dawg-bite!" he exclaimed joyously. "Well I'm from there, too. Texas! That's where I'm from! You just come on with me! I-jest-be-dawg!"

Grasping my arm he enthusiastically escorted me through the crowd to where his wife sat intensely watching the hordes of black Africans passing to and fro.

"Mother!" the Texas man exulted, "Why, Mother, this here man is one of us! Dawg-bite-if-he-ain't!" He was almost dancing with satisfaction as he thrust me toward the startled white woman who seemed already overwhelmed by the blackness surrounding her. She looked pleadingly into her husband's eyes as if to remind him that this was not his first rumpling of her sense of self.

Finally she said, "Well, I don't *know*, Albert," carefully folding her hands and shrinking deeper into the security of her plastic chair. "When will our plane be leaving?"

The bubble of euphoria burst. Dog-bite if it didn't!

During World War II, when all travel below the Mason-Dixon Line was still rigidly segregated, I had another dining-car experience that was considerably less innocuous. Proudly wearing the uniform of the United States Navy I traveled from the East Coast to San Diego on a train carrying German prisoners of war into the western interior of the country. The Germans had the run of the diner, but because I was black, whenever I went there to eat I had to be seated behind a curtain lest my presence, even in the military uniform of my country, offend the honor and spoil the appetites of our Caucasian guests from Nazi Germany, whose mission and whose intention was to destroy us.

Racial presumption is such a powerful cultural residuum that long after social and moral reforms have taken place, it sometimes triggers quixotic expressions or behavior which would be humorous were it not for their tragic implications. After the war I returned to school and eventually wound up in graduate school at Boston University, where once again I encountered the tender innocence of a racist child who had been taught to despise and hate black people, but with a dignified show of courtesy and good manners. I lived at the time in a university apartment complex for graduate students at 14 Buswell Street. One Saturday morning

I returned from the grocery store to find a little blonde-haired girl straining valiantly to reach the button on the elevator. "Would you like me to push it for you?" I asked.

"No!" she protested. "No! I want to do it for myself. Lift me up and I will do it." I set my groceries down and did as I was asked. "Thank you very much," she said sweetly as the elevator rumbled toward the ground floor. Then she added as a sort of afterthought, "But I don't like you 'cause you're black!"

"Oh, I don't think you mean that," I said and offered her an apple from my bag of groceries.

"Thank you very much," she said with the graciousness of a little cherub. "But I still don't like you because you're black! *You're black all over!* And your hands are black!" With that she threw the unbitten apple on the floor and ran up the stairs, leaving the elevator to me and my blackness. All over.

In the summer of 1986 Duke University Dean of the Chapel Robert "Bob" Young and I went on a fishing trip in rural South Carolina. Just before dark in the midst of a rainstorm we were deposited by friends at a remote cabin on a remote lake deep in a forest in an area unfamiliar to either of us. Late that same night, at the height of the storm, Dr. Young had a heart attack. I was faced with the necessity of getting emergency attention for a very sick white man in rural South Carolina in the middle of a very dark and stormy night. It turned out to be quite an adventure.

It took three hours to find our way out of the woods and into a town where there was a hospital. Everybody we approached regarded us with suspicion, and at one isolated farmhouse the dogs were released and I was waved off with a shotgun. We finally found a small hospital and Bob was admitted there about three o'clock in the morning. I went up to his floor and asked to see him before calling his wife back in Durham.

"Now what might you want?" the elderly white nurse on duty asked testily when I approached the nurse's station.

"I'd like to see Reverend Robert Young," I said. "I'd like to speak with him for a moment if that is possible."

"Well, now, you can't do that," the nurse said. "Why, if you talking about the preacher they brought in here, well he's done been placed in intensive care, and can't nobody see him but a member of his family."

"Well, that's me, I'm a member of his family," I said, letting myself in under the generic wire. "I'm the only member of his family here."

"Well Lord-a-mercy!" she exclaimed looking intently at my face. "Just how in the world could that be?" she wondered aloud. "Why no wonder he's so sick. Why that there preacher, he's done been sick a long, long time, and I reckon the doctor's gonna be sick too when he finds out what room I put him in. My-Lord-a-mercy!"

Many of the behaviors I encountered coming through the fire are no longer in vogue, of course, but the spirit that gave those behaviors currency lives on and continues to express itself in ways that are as destructive of character and community as ever. The notion of race and place remains deeply embedded in the American psyche and is an inevitable concomitant to every aspect of American life. This book begins by relating a spectrum of the racial experiences that plowed the ground of my personal consciousness and planted there the seeds of a conventional interpretation of reality by which I was expected to live. Or die. I did not, could not, and do not accept that interpretation as either final or creditable, and the remainder of the book is a series of selective responses to those conventional realities across a lifetime of unremitting challenge.

However, this book does not intend to be an autobiography— certainly not in the conventional sense. While the selected experiences shared here are quite real and are intrinsic to my personal sense of identity and significance as a human being, they are not the *sum* of my life. There is a great deal more to the privilege of matriculating reality than the underside of the human predicament. Throughout the centuries-long rape of Africa, somewhere flowers bloomed, music played, and the awesome majesty of Kilimanjaro bore compelling testimony of the judiciousness of survival. When the savagery of Aryanism eclipsed a thousand years of German civilization in a spasm of unspeakable horror, neither the Jews in the death camps nor the directing Nazi Germans were ready to raze the cathedrals or the synagogues and capitulate to the inevitable triumph of evil. The triumph of evil is never inevitable until the resuscitation of good has been abandoned. Life is episodic, and it encompasses multiple planes of experience. The trick is to coordinate and integrate the diversity so as to produce maximum clarity and meaning, or living is reduced to mere existence—a concatenation of spasms in the flux. There is an aspect of the human spirit which recognizes something *beyond* the exigency of the moment; something *beyond* the rape of Africa; *beyond* the holocaust of Nazi chauvinism and genocide. And there is something beyond the agony and the ignominy, the destructiveness and the sheer inconvenience of race and place in the United States. And while I do indeed commit myself irrevocably to the search for the realization of the promise of what must be beyond what has been and what now is, what I say here is hardly biography because it is addressed essentially to but a single syndrome of the human predicament. True biography searches out the integrality of a significant life, and from the sum, the total experience reflected through the prism of history, we may derive new insights for other lives in the process of becoming. I have no such ambitions, and the commentary which follows is but another dimension of my response to the presumptions that would hold me hostage in my own camp.

There may be an element of catharsis, and sometimes even humor, in the retelling of the racial slurs that have been transcended and the slights that have been overcome, for twice-told tales that end in "success" have a way of trivializing the horror that made them worth telling. Nevertheless, the catharsis is fleeting, and the humor shared under the most benign circumstances does not always narcotize the dismay that begins deep in the recesses of the soul, beyond the acquittal of the intellect or the healing erosions that chasten the memory. The pain often endures, despite the best intentions of social lobotomy, for the scars are still there, and sometimes the flesh beneath them festers.

What lies ahead is an attempt to add perspective to raw experience. The practice of racism is not an abstraction; it produces patterns of behavior which involve real people in highly stressful conflicts of interests and expectation. Nor can one "stand outside the self," as it were, and learn very much about what is going on. The individual self is too involved. The self is a part of the problem—a critical component in the maintenance of an ethos that shapes the society the way it is. The stakes—the investments in the game—are high, so high that serious, constructive, open-minded dialogue between the parties of disparate interests is seldom attempted. Transsocial conversation in America is either trivial and inane or vengeful and vindictive. It is done primarily in the courts or in other areas of adversarial association. In consequence, nobody knows what it's like to be socially confined except those who are, and that is the way the strategy of confinement is ordered. Perhaps Americans would change our ways if we could see a little more clearly in juxtaposition to each other, and if we could bring ourselves to speak candidly about what we see.

Just the other day the Honorable Newt Gingrich, the Republican Speaker of the House of Representatives, leaked the information that all African Americans have to do to be accepted is be successful. "Nobody would object if General Colin Powell moved next door," Mr. Gingrich opined. One wonders how a man smart enough and "successful" enough to have serious aspirations for the American presidency could be so droll, except that Mr. Gingrich's selective naïveté is strictly in keeping with the need not to know that keeps the system intact. Such political pundits need fear no enlightenment from the universities, where "learning" is even more selective than what the politicians know; nor yet from the churches, where an "apology for the racism of our fathers" is somehow expected to exonerate this generation from the consequences of *its* behavior. Nevertheless, the Southern Baptists who made that gesture by public resolution have at least put themselves on the record for *thinking* about the problem, and that suggests that they just may have caught a vision of what must lie beyond our present intransigence. If there is such a vision, it is a vision I share, and the essays which follow are addressed to its realization.

Because the notion of race and place saturates American life,

every serious human response is ultimately a racial response because the problem to which it is addressed is almost certain to
be rooted in the infrastructure of the American commitment to a
pervasive doctrine of race and place. Hence, whether one is concerned about the plight of young black males, the responsibilities
of thinking, the possibilities of justice, or the meaning of identity, that concern will be shaped and conditioned in the peculiar
mix of conventions which structure our values and dictate the
politics of our response. *The specter of race will out!* And if it is
not determinative, it will be the critical factor in the process of
determination.

II

THE FIRE
IN
ALABAMA

What is black

What is white

What does it mean

To be American?

—C. ERIC LINCOLN,

This Road since Freedom

THE NOTION OF RACE

I don't know precisely when it was that I was first aware of *race* as a factor in all of the meaningful experiences in my life. Race as a matter of physical differentiation I knew and understood, of course, almost from the moment of self-awareness. People were physiologically different, even in my own family. Some were tall, some short; some fat, some lean; some had pronounced cheekbones, others had more rounded faces. Some were box-ankled, pigeon-toed, slew-footed, or bowlegged; some were light-skinned, some were dark, but all were family. Family to love and be loved by. If I thought about race at all, I'm sure I thought about it as an extension of "family." I saw people on the street who were taller and shorter, lighter and darker than the folks at home, but it never occurred to me that because they were not the precise clones of the people I played with and ate with and went to church with, they were, or wanted to be considered a totally different order of beings, *a people apart*. That didn't make sense. People are just people—no more, no less. How can there be a people apart from people?

But the day did come—inevitably, I know now—when the notion of race as a factor of irreconcilable difference came suddenly into my limited experience and fixed itself in the middle of my being like some slithering, menacing, irrefragable, insatiable ogre, feeding on my consciousness and dripping with a venom that poisoned everything it touched. And there, unbidden, it fixed itself, and I became an involuntary clone of all those other millions of Americans for whom that insidious intruder is a silent partner to every personal relationship; the first and final appeal to every meaningful human evaluation. The notion of race is the hydra-headed monster which stifles our most beautiful dreams before they are fairly dreamt, calling us away from the challenges of normative human interaction to a dissonance of suspicion and hatred in pursuit of a fantasy that never was. Race is a cultural fiction. It is an emotional crutch for people whose sense of personal adequacy is threatened. It is the joker in a deck stacked for personal advantage in a game of life where the dealer must always win to break even. But in the world of objective reality, the alleged pure and definable race does not exist. There are no master races, no inferior races—only individuals and groups of *people* who in the peculiar accidents of personal existence are more or less disadvantaged, or more or less advantaged than some of their fellows, irrespective of what they look like before breakfast. All cats look gray in the dark. And so long as men and women locate the initiative for their existence beyond themselves, and the contingency for their survival in each other, so long will the proposition on the color of cats and the uniformity of the human species hold true.

Whatever the rational and moral conclusions about race, most unfortunately, the best data the sciences can produce have not solved the persistent problem of racism. If race does not exist in reality, it exists with the *force* of reality and the *consequences* of reality in the minds of enough Americans to seriously qualify most orders of relationships between groups and among individuals. Racism is oblivious of the prescriptions of religion and the proscriptions of law alike. I am a case in point. So are you. There are few people in America who are not in the course of any given day given a *racial* appraisal which dramatically affects the course and the quality of their personal lives and the nature of their relationships with other human beings. Your job or profession, your neighborhood, your church or school, your credit at the bank, your opportunity for public service, your likelihood of going to jail would perhaps all be different from their present realities except for the notion of *race*. So, indeed, would mine.

I have not undertaken this recounting because it contains any new truths or profound illuminations. There is a need for it, however, and the need is primarily my own. It is a private need. It is a need to review the objective authority of science, the moral authority of the human endowment, and the accumulations of long years of personal experience lest in the persuasive rhetoric of race and place, I forget near the end the hard-learned lessons of the beginning and wander off into the wilderness of abject despair. Yes, it is a need to recall past experiences that may call for reinterpretation by a more mature and synoptic vision. It is an excursion of catharsis and purgation, for the sediments of racial slander and rebuff have a way of accumulating in the soul and festering. It is a part of the continuing search for truth and understanding, whatever the cost, that every responsible human being is required to indulge all life long; it is the dogged hope that still gropes for the latch which may open up the extraordinary treasures of true community, which always seems to lie just beyond the next illusion. We know that truth is always there before our eyes, but the vicissitudes of living so often obscure it, or distort our perception of it. Nor do we always want to find the truth even as we search for it, for truth is freedom, and freedom is responsibility, and in the absence of altruistic intent it is burdensome beyond the casual limits of endurance. Even so. We ought to search about from time to time that the mind might be refreshed, the vision refocused, and the resolution to extract from life its true essence rather than its excreta be reconfirmed in the effort.

ALABAMA: THE TENDER YEARS

I shall always be sentimental about Alabama. It used to be my home. There were cotton fields and clay pits; and an abandoned limestone quarry where we swam in the summertime. And there were dusty roads like velvet to the tough soles of our bare feet. And creeks full of perch. And peach orchards to rob. And snakes not to step on. And county fairs once a year. And on Sunday mornings there was the wonderful smell of frying chicken—to be ready with lots of rice and turnip greens when the preacher came by to eat dinner after service. And there was the procession to the Sunday school that began at Miss Katie's house and grew by ones and twos and threes all the way to Village View Methodist Church on the corner of Hines Street and Plato Jones Dirt Road.

It was just a little town in north Alabama. So small that when anybody left to go to Nashville or Chicago, everybody missed him before the train had whistled on past the county line. Athens wasn't much of a town, but that's where I was born, and there is a part of me still there, left over from those tender years.

The first consciousness of race comes early. It is not something you learn in the same way you learn about stinging caterpillars or poison ivy. You do not have to learn it from some overt experience. It is a pervasive awareness, an insidious thing that seeps into the soil of consciousness, sending its toxic tendrils deep into the walls of the mind. It is like a mold, a blight. If you scrape it away here, you find it mockingly virulent there. Once the concept of race takes root in the mind, it is there to stay. You cannot run away from it because it is *inside* you. You cannot close your eyes to it because it is an idée fixe that never leaves the retina of awareness. You may cover it with an intellectual tarpaulin as you would cover a weed patch on an otherwise perfect lawn with a sheet of black plastic. But the landscape is marred by the patchwork, and when it is removed, the weeds you thought were dead come springing back to life.

In the South, where I was raised, the pervasive awareness of race was helped along by a series of "lessons" learned in the process of growing up. These lessons were sometimes impromptu, and often impersonal, but they were never unplanned or unintended. They were always there in the arsenal of race and place waiting for the most effective moment for inculcation. Their sources were varied, and as might be expected some of the most traumatic derived from everyday personal relations with white people. But others were carefully taught at home or in the informal councils of the elders as the fundamentals of black survival. Some were taught in more stressful settings by the local police or by night riders as constant reminders of the inevitability of the status quo, white over black, now and forever. And no nonsense about it. Depending upon the source and cause of such "instruction," the lessons were often accompanied by loss of employment, foreclosure, loss of credit or credibility, intimidation, personal assault, jail time, a "bad name," or any combination of these. Repeated failure to learn meant long-term incarceration or permanent exile. Peremptory challenge meant death.

A FIRST LESSON

The summer when I was nine years old I went to the county health office in the basement of the county courthouse to be immunized against some childhood disease. As I stood in a long line of children, waiting for my turn at the needle, I became aware that some of the boys and girls were not required to wait in line. These favored children, who were taken as soon as they came into the room, were all "white." I was vaguely aware, of course, that they were somehow different beyond the fact of their whiteness, for this uncanny, unexplained awareness is the first bitter fruit of acculturation. But I had, as yet, no appreciation of the deadly meaning of that difference. I had swum and fished and fought and filched and played with anybody who would play, white or black. What did it matter, if you could hit the ball and run the bases? As often as not my playmates and fellow adventurers had been white, for these were the children who owned the baseballs, the bicycles, the air rifles, and all the other toys and paraphernalia that enhanced the fun and adventure to which every boy seemed somehow entitled. Most of the time white boys and black boys played together without incident. The major problem for black children was managing to escape from the ever-escalating chores of the household, not the acceptance of the white children waiting to play with them. My grandmother cooked for a white family, and I had always felt at ease anywhere in the town. People *knew* her because she "cooked for the Martins." And I guess I expected to be known and accepted by extension. How, then, could I have known that I was about to challenge one of the fundamental privileges of white identity when I presented myself unbidden to be serviced? *I was nine years old:* How could I have known that this instance of tending two races at the same time in the same place was itself an extraordinary concession to expediency in protecting the town from some sort of epidemic? How could I have known that had we been adults instead of children such a breach of convention could not have happened if the whole town had been dying of cholera or whatever, expediency notwithstanding?

I could not have known any of this, so in my childish determination to enter into the spirit of the game the white kids seemed to be playing, I stepped forward with some newly arrived white children and offered my arm without being specifically bidden to do so. The very next second I learned my first lesson in race relations. The nurse grabbed my outstretched arm and flung me brutally back against the wall. "Boy!" she scowled threateningly, "Get back in line! *Get all the way back there! All you niggers have to wait!*" It was brutal, it was direct. And it was perplexing. As I stood against the wall rubbing my arm, I soon came to realize that it was not my arm that was hurting, it was my soul. There was a sort of numbness, a *dead* feeling. The pain was *inside* me and I would never be able to rub it away. Over and over I repeated the words: *Get all the way back there! All niggers have to wait! All niggers have to wait! All niggers have to wait! All niggers have to wait! Wait! Wait! Wait! Nigger, wait!*

My first lesson was a difficult one, for it offered no explanation, no rationale. Just, "*All niggers have to wait.*" Why? For what? I did not know that the *why* had already been answered, and that I was supposed to know the answer. It was presumed to be innate in my being. Ultimately, the answer was enured in the color of my skin. That was *why,* and I was supposed to know that. The question *for what?* was endless in application: for an education, for a job, for a place to live, for a ride on the bus, for a space on the elevator, for a place to go to school, for buying a loaf of bread, for ginning a load of cotton, for a chance to vote, for justice in the courts, and even for a chance to fight for the homeland. I was supposed to know that too. *All niggers have to wait!* and since I was obviously a nigger in the mind of the nurse, I was charged with knowing all that by the ripe old age of nine.

The next lesson in race relations came close on the heels of the first, and this time it was learned not in the strange, unpredictable world of the white man but from the lips of my own grandmother. It was a curious lesson indeed, and one I was not to fully understand until succeeding years unlocked the remarkable esoterics of history and economics that structured the South in confusing paradox. It happened this way:

I lived with my grandparents on the edge of town in a frame house on Westview Street. It wasn't much of a street, really, and when it rained too hard it was impassable to all except the most determined pedestrian traffic. Yet we were only two blocks from the edge of the white community — "where the sidewalk begins" — and scarcely eight or ten blocks from Courthouse Square, the center of the town itself. Horses and wagons were still common in the town, and indeed they remain so in gardening and small-scale farming to this day.

One rainy Saturday morning a white man knocked at our door and asked to borrow a singletree. He explained that his wagon, loaded with firewood, was stuck in the mud a little way down the street, and he had broken his singletree in his efforts to dislodge it. My grandfather had a horse and wagon which he used for odd jobs of gardening and hauling about town, and for "farming" his three acres of cotton. As he was sick in bed, I offered to fetch the "tree," whereupon Grandma ordered me into the house and directed the white man to the barn to find the piece for himself. Then she immediately dispatched me behind him to make certain that he made no unauthorized acquisitions. When the man brought the singletree back half an hour later, he again knocked at the front door. However, Grandma refused to answer the door, and a "look" from her conveyed perfectly the message that I had better not answer it either.

A few minutes later the white man went around the house and knocked on the back door. Ma Matt immediately got out of her rocking chair, smoothed out her apron, and went to open the kitchen door.

"Yes?" she said.

"I brought back your 'tree," the man said. "I got my wagon out of that mudhole, and A'nty, I'm much obliged to you."

My grandmother was not a black-skinned woman, but at that moment her face darkened so that I became a little frightened. I had never seen her so angry.

"What did you say?" she demanded. "Didn't you call me 'A'nty'?" She shook the heavy singletree at the man, who retreated rapidly across the back porch and down the low steps to the ground. "Well, I ain't your A'nty!" she declared. "And if you don't know your manners no better than that, then you get on out of this yard right now!" With that she threw the "tree" at the man and he hurried out of the yard and down the street to his wagon. Had not Grandpa appeared at the door to see what the commotion was about I'm certain she would have chased that white man all the way to the pavement!

When Mama Matt had had a chance to cool off a little, I asked her why she had become so angry.

"Didn't you hear that white man call me 'A'nty'?" she asked disdainfully. Her face was starting to darken up again.

"Yes ma'am," I answered hastily. Then, with well-calculated innocence I ventured: "But the people you work for, Miss Lidie and Mr. Martin, they call you 'A'nty'?"

"Yes!" she said sharply, "but *he* ain't Miss Lidie and he ain't Mr. Dubbie Gee. He ain't nothing but a po' white cracker, and ain't no po' white trash, gon' come up in my yard and call me no 'A'nty!' *Po' white trash don't count for nothin!*"

This was indeed a strange world, and it was growing increasingly complex by the day. I had hardly learned that there are important distinctions between white people and people who are not white before I was required to learn a second lesson—that not all white people are the same. *Po' white trash don't count!* They could be required to come to the back door, just like colored people had to go to the back doors of the "quality" white folks downtown. And you could say "yes" to them, though to "real" white folks you had to say "Yes sir!" and "Yes ma'am!" You could even chase them away from your house if they insulted you by calling you "A'nty," which was considered an honorific if used by *quality* white people. Later I was to hear Mr. Martin refer to poor white folks like the woodman as "pore-assed peckerwoods"; and many times I heard him tell Grandpa that "one good nigger is worth half-a-dozen of them redneck crackers spitting 'round Courthouse Square on Saturday." Later, I was to hear him elaborate on just what a "good nigger" was, and that would be another lesson in the race relations everybody was supposed to understand.

COUNTING COTTON MONEY

The town in which I lived did not afford a public high school that black people could attend. There were two public high schools for white youngsters, but as far as the city fathers and the county administration was concerned, education for black children should not exceed the sixth grade, especially if higher education for Blacks meant scaled-down appropriations for white schools. And of course, for black and white children to attend the same school was a notion beyond the possibility of conception in the Alabama of that era.

There was, however, a private high school for Blacks in the town. It was a missionary school, established by the New England–based American Missionary Association shortly after the Civil War. And it was a better school than any the city might have provided had it had a mind to do so. Very possibly it was the best school in north Alabama. It was run as a missionary expression of the Congregational church, and its interracial faculty was disproportionately blessed with dedicated Christian women from Massachusetts and Connecticut.

Tuition at Trinity High School was twenty-seven dollars a year, but since no one ever had twenty-seven dollars to pay in a lump sum, tuition was computed at three dollars a month. Even this sum was difficult to come by, so more than half of the student body were either working for the school or were on scholarships provided by New England philanthropy. As for myself, I first started earning my tuition when I reached the third grade by hauling horse manure from Grandpa's stable to spread on the school garden at fifteen cents per wheelbarrow load. Then, when I was thirteen, our home burned to the ground; Grandpa was sick again; there was no money in the house. Mama Matt and I went out into the nearby fields where the cotton had been harvested, and after several hours of effort managed to "glean" a large sackful of cotton "lint." School was open . . . and I had to have books. And books cost money if you went to a black school.

Early next morning I put the sack of cotton on a wheelbarrow and pushed it into town to the gin. The manager of the gin was a tall red-faced man who always wore a cigar stub plugged into the corner of his mouth. I had seen him before when I had gone there with Grandpa, but I had never spoken to him. I did not know his name, but he was standing in the doorway of his office as I pushed the wheelbarrow upon the platform.

"What you got there, boy?" he asked as he wobbled the cigar stub from corner to corner of his small, tobacco-stained mouth.

"I've got some cotton I'd like to sell," I said.

"You steal it, nigger?" he demanded. When I assured him I did not, he ordered me to "put it on the scales."

I hung the bag on the long iron balance that is a symbol of cotton country all over the South. The white man adjusted the pea, and when the balance was struck I could see that the bag of cotton weighed exactly forty-one pounds. Cotton lint was selling at nine cents a pound. Allowing a pound for the bag, I made the calculation that I would receive three dollars and sixty cents. I would use part of the money to buy something to take home for breakfast. The rest would go for books and tuition. My musings were interrupted by the white man's order to dump the cotton into a bin he pointed out to me. I did so. When I emptied the bag, I rolled it carefully and followed the white man upstairs into his office to be paid. I was very proud to be taking home some money so that my family could eat again. Suddenly, I was the man of the house. Ma Matt would be mighty proud of me.

The white man sat down behind a battered old desk and busied himself with some papers. I waited with a carefully controlled impatience, for I wanted very much to be able to get on home in time to go to the store for Mama Matt before going to school. At last the man looked up as if he was surprised to see anyone standing there. He seemed very annoyed, and the cigar stump wobbled back and forth around his mouth like a bottle stopper on a trotline.

"What'cha want, boy?" he asked in the suspicious, measured tones of someone about to make trouble.

I told him that I was waiting to be paid for my cotton. "What you mean you waitin' to get your money?" he rasped. "Boy, I thought I done paid you." His cold blue eyes glinted in the early morning light. When I showed no sign of leaving, he felt around in his pocket and flipped a coin in my direction. Instinctively, I caught it. It was a quarter. The white man again busied himself among the papers on his desk. He was as oblivious of my presence as he was of Tutankamen. I was standing there in front of him—close enough to touch him—but suddenly I felt as though I did not exist at all. And at that moment I did not want to exist. I wanted to disintegrate, to wither away into the nothingness he communicated that I was. I was ashamed. Humiliated. And I was afraid. Somehow I knew that I had unwittingly stepped across a boundary. I tried to move. Perhaps if I could move my feet I could somehow pass into the nothingness I coveted to save me from the awesome sense of developing catastrophe. Finally I stumbled out of the office on leaden feet, but by the time I had reached the ground, my feet wouldn't go any further. I turned and forced myself back up the stairs and into the office.

"Excuse me, sir," I said without waiting to see if anybody was listening. "Excuse me, but I think you made a mistake. I had forty pounds of cotton and that was just a quarter you gave me." Suddenly, there was an awesome silence; a dreadful eternity in which there was absolutely no sound at all. *Anywhere.* The world had simply stopped moving, stopped *existing!* And then just as suddenly, I could hear again.

"Jist wait a minute, nigger," the gin man said very slowly and carefully. "Jist a minute." He got up and slouched to the door of his office and bolted it. Then he came and planted himself in front of me like some glowering colossus from Hell. "Now, nigger," he demanded with the greasy unction of an executioner, "what's that you said? I done made a mistake? That's what you said? Well I'll jist be goddamned and a sonofabitch to boot! Nigger done come ra'chere in my office an' done called me a lie ra'chere to my face!"

The truth is that I had no intention of such a gross breach of manners as calling an adult, *any* adult, a liar. Grandma would not have stood for that even if I survived it. At the moment I was only thinking about the books I needed to get back in school, and of something for Mama Matt and Papa to eat until Mama Matt got her wash money on the weekend. But because it was true that I was proud to have a quick mind with figures, I think that somehow I had actually expected the gin man to be pleased I was able to help him settle the matter so quickly. Now, as it turned out, that "quick mind" my teachers applauded and my grandmother expected was about to cost me my life. Nor was my premonition of impending catastrophe merely the excess of boyish imagination. The precedents were all around me as elements of daily experience, and a fleeting recollection of a prayer in a poem by Langston Hughes fluttered into my consciousness:

> O Lord if you can save me from this man
> Don't let him make a pulp out of me
> But the Lord, He was not quick
> And the man raised up his stick. . . .
> And he beat the living hell out of me.[1]

The angry white man stood looking down at me, his red, bony fists tightly balled and hanging tensed at his side. He was tall, the tallest man I ever saw, and I felt so very small at thirteen years old. "Now, nigger, I want you to tell me one more time what you said to me so's I can be shore I done got it right."

I wanted desperately to apologize, or to at least find some more acceptable words to tell the man what he owed me. But no other words would come. There were no other words, and so I heard myself explaining: "You see sir, I had forty pounds of cotton, not counting the croker sack I brought it in. I see on the wall there that your price is nine cents a pound. That comes to $3.60 for the forty pounds, sir, but you only gave me a quarter."

"And you say I done made a mistake? Near as I can figger it, you done called me a lie!" The man flushed red to the base of his neck. He spat out the cigar stub and his lips jerked and sputtered wordlessly, tobacco juice oozing from the corner of his mouth. Suddenly I saw his red, bony fist coming up at me, but I was too paralyzed with fear to move. His first blow to my chin lifted me off the floor and crumpled me at his feet. Then he began to rhythmically stomp my head and kick me in the face and stom-

1. Langston Hughes, "Who But the Lord," in *The Panther and the Lash* (New York: Alfred A. Knopf, 1974).

ach with his heavy brogans. Each kick was punctuated with an oath. "A goddamned nigger!" he complained, "'A coming in here gon' teach me how to count cotton money! A goddamned, black-assed nigger gon' tell me I done made a mistake! Iggernant-assed nigger gon' try to count behind a white man! Boy you listen and you listen good: *Aint no nigger can count behind a white man!* God ain't made no such-a nigger yet, and God ain't gon' never make no such-a nigger because ain't no such-a nigger can be made! And don't you never forget it!"

That lesson in racial etiquette cost me a tooth, a bloated, bloody face, a ruptured stomach, and a mouth full of scar tissue. The lesson was indelible: *Ain't no nigger can count behind a white man!* The lesson was explicit, and though I have never been impressed by the credibility of its source, I have never forgotten it. Nevertheless, it was always a confusing proposition. If the white man's figures on cotton money are not ever to be challenged, is *all* white thinking beyond debate? Theology? Ethics? Law? Art? Politics? It was a disturbing prospect that I thought left all civilization a little more vulnerable to the arbitrariness of racially selective perception than seems warranted by what we know of human fallibility.

SEX FORSOOTH

The American South represents the most intricate social complex in the modern world. Many of its conventions and behaviors exhibit a tentativeness that is altogether baffling to the "outsider" not conditioned to its peculiar order of personal relations. But these "personal relations" always refer to an implicit understanding about the Negro's "place," that is, the peculiar limitations of the alleged black joie de vivre in respect to the unrestricted prerogatives of white people.

Sex is the most critical and the most volatile area. Here it is that an unchallenged sophistry most often takes over the rational mind and reverses the calendar of human evolution to a pristine state of nature. Sex is the ultimate reason behind all the anti-reason that makes racism ludicrous. For centuries intermarriage has been the supreme tabu of all social intercourse, the horrible specter that haunted the most casual social contacts, the incubus that stalked the elaborate boudoirs of the big house while the gentlemen sworn to protect the big house boudoirs were out stalking the slave cabins. Who can understand it except to sense intuitively that the whole body of politics, law, economics, religion, and whatever else that could be brought to focus on "the Negro Problem" seemed somehow to be focused on a problem that was "Negro" only by the courtesy of casuistry?

My grandmother was a unique weld of self-respect adjusted to what she could not hope to successfully overcome in this life. She was able to maintain a certain dignity and appreciation of her own worth without incurring the destructive notice of those forces overtly in control of her destiny. Survival, that was the first order of business. Creative survival, if you could manage it. But *dignity,* whatever else, for survival without dignity was mere existence, a hapless state unworthy of the effort. This was no mean achievement, but she was able to avoid most of the self-consuming frustration that is the corollary of living in a caste-oriented society. Ma Matt acknowledged no "place," even though she knew that a "place" had been thrust upon her. With the assortment of children, grandchildren, and the children of nobody in particular who were lucky enough to live with her seated on the floor about her knees in front of the fire, she read the Bible and taught us that we were "all God's chillun, *and as good as anybody!*" And we had better act like it! *All the time.* She couldn't beat the system, and she knew it, but she constantly resisted it at those points where reprisal would likely be less than absolute. Mama Matt knew, for example, that the "poor whites" were not a controlling factor in the system, and that they were despised and exploited by the "good" white folks she knew, but they were white just the same, *and not black.* A crucial difference. But poor whites didn't count for much in the conventional equation of race and place, and any unwarranted assumption of prerogative on their part could be successfully denied, thus retrieving a little personal dignity from the whites who held it hostage. All white people were not the same, but they all got the same message if you wrote it right.

But Grandma also knew how far she could go. She knew that living among the *real* white folks, the power elite, required a certain degree of patterned conformity, and that both she and those dependent upon her were required to make this obeisance or suffer the direst of consequences. So she taught us to say "yes *ma'am*" and "yes *sir,*" but as a courtesy to which *all* adults were entitled. Nor were we ever to "talk back" to an adult, *any* adult. I would be punished quite as severely, and perhaps more so, for a discourtesy to an adult in my own black community as for not minding my manners downtown. Respect was due everybody respectable, *white folks included,* and when it was an ingrained aspect of personality, the lapse that could cost you your life was unlikely to occur.

Yet there were areas of specific application, areas where the wisdom acquired from a lifetime spent in learning the ways of white folks admonished her to tread carefully. Here she taught us as if in preparation for a sojourn in an alien land. And if we asked the *why* of this or that, she would only reply that "when it comes time, you'll know why." She spoke with the voice of prophecy.

One of the more curious of these teachings had to do with my going into town. I realize now that as I evolved into a teenager, my grandmother grew increasingly apprehensive about my going to town, especially on Saturdays, when large numbers of rural whites and Blacks from the surrounding country came to see the sights and visit with each other around Courthouse Square. Eventually, the matter came to a point where she preferred trudging into town on Saturdays herself rather than having me go down for her as I had always done. On occasions when necessity demanded that I go, she would give me specific instructions: "Go on down, tend to your business, *and come on back, directly!*" And as I grew older she began to conclude with, "And son, don't you go down there looking at them old country gals' legs. Just mind your business and come on home."

It eventually dawned upon me that she meant *white* country girls, and by extension, *all* white girls. This was, of course, an instance of one of her general admonitions with a specific application. I had played, as a child, with whites and Blacks of both sexes indiscriminately. But such contacts with the white children came gradually to an end at about the age of eleven or twelve, and I had given it no conscious thought since then. It seemed a natural development of growing up, but nobody ever said why. But Ma Matt left nothing to chance. She knew a lot about social cause and effect from firsthand experience. *She* knew why.

Ma Matt was not alone in her concern that the white man feel secure in an area where he has always seemed to feel most threatened. There was also Miss Allyn, redoubtable principal of Trinity School for more than thirty years. Miss Louise Hurlbutt Allyn was a Connecticut Yankee, and a more noble Christian woman never sacrificed marriage and family for the cause of black education and uplift. During her three decades in Alabama she too became an intuitive observer of the strange ways of white folk, and she was instructed by what she saw, her own whiteness notwithstanding. Trinity School had already had the distinction of being burned to the ground once by a white mob determined to bring a peremptory halt to the education of Negroes in Limestone County. If history should repeat itself, who could say whether another school could ever be built?

Her school was an entryway that must be kept open at all costs. Deep in the pragmatics of the Yankee mentality was the firm conviction that education was the *only* key capable of unlocking Africans' potential for the mature religious understanding which could in time prepare them for responsible moral behavior and political responsibility. So with the patience born of dedication to her Christian responsibility as she saw it, Miss Allyn left to history the questions of lesser significance. Thus she could with equanimity enroll in her school countless children who lacked a proper surname because their fathers were white. The surname of the mother would suffice. And she could counsel her bigger boys, as often she did when they were required to do an errand downtown, to "avert the eyes lest they compromise the soul!" And they did, or at least they tried, because they trusted this white Yankee who had cast her lot among them. *Avert the eyes!* A phraseology I learned from Miss Allyn as I did so many poetic and romantic phrases, but the lesson intended I had already learned at home from Ma Matt. *Avert the eyes!* It was not only the soul that was in danger of being compromised; survival itself was at stake.

In North Carolina during the early nervousness of World War II a black man was reportedly jailed and fined for "assault" because he *looked* at a white woman who passed along the street. And in Selma, Alabama, a black man was jailed for painting his own house from a ladder that permitted him to see a white woman sunbathing on her lawn half a block away. I do not know if these men's souls were compromised by what they saw, but in failing to *avert the eyes* their freedom was taken away and a new term, "reckless eyeballing," found its way into the folklore of the black experience.

NIGGEROLOGY

The next lesson in my life course was extracted from the dubious sagacity of the choleric old curmudgeon I worked for as a boy, Mr. "Dubbie Gee" Martin. Mr. Martin was a tangled mass of contradictions. Often kind and generous in his way, he seemed almost driven to make it clear that "his way" implied no license for the slightest abuse of the conventions of race and place. Although he ran a small dairy in which I worked as bottle washer and delivery boy, his principal occupation was managing a commissary store which supplied the needs of most of the sharecroppers and field hands in the county, most of whom were Negroes. It was in that capacity that he claimed to know more about "niggers," his favorite topic of discourse, "than their own mammies what brought 'em into this world. Man and boy," he would tell you, "I been handlin' niggers longer than I been pissin' off myself; and I can tell you right now that no matter where you get 'em from, there ain't a dime's worth of difference in a boatload. I ain't got a thing in the world against the colored race," he'd tell you, "but a nigger is going to be just that, because that's what Almighty God intended him to be, a nigger!"

According to Mr. Martin, Negroes were all alike because they shared a common racial geniture characterized by many pronounced and obvious limitations when compared with white people. But within the fixed limitations that set them apart they did have a crude set of dispositions which distinguished one from another, enabling some discretion in the matter of utility and management. So it turned out that although all Negroes were the same, there were different degrees of sameness. About that Mr. Dubbie Gee was emphatic, and usually profanely so. *All niggers are the same; variations on a theme of niggerness!*

Now, Mr. Martin's choice of language was not necessarily intended by him to be pejorative; it was merely a shorthand convenience for describing "what anybody but a baboon could see for himself." On occasion he'd use the phrase "colored person" to refer to someone he particularly liked or "respected," but in the final analysis, to his mind even the best colored person in the world was ultimately just a good nigger with "a whole lot of motherwit." For example, I think he had a genuine, albeit quixotic affection for my grandfather, who had worked for him for thirty years or more. He never to my knowledge called Papa a nigger to his face or by direct reference, but inevitably he must have included him in his general references to that alien race of dark-skinned African people he found so amusing, so exasperating, so predictable, and so necessary. Mr. Martin could not imagine life without niggers, and since they were inevitable, he considered it a matter of common expedience to know what to expect of them. Hence, he had developed his own science of niggerology, which he used like an Etruscan bed, lopping off some here, stretching some there to achieve a common fit for all. Since I rode with him delivering the milk two or three hours every day, I got the full benefit of his findings, gratuitously.

Niggers, according to Mr. Martin, came in three designations: "good niggers," "bad niggers," and "smart niggers." There was nothing that disturbed him more than a bad nigger unless it was a smart nigger. By the same token there was nothing that delighted him more than a good nigger. Mr. Martin laid it down in his lexicon that every nigger was either good, bad, or smart; although some of the smart niggers were also "slick," that is, cunning and deceitful. Every nigger had an element of slickness in him, but in the smart nigger it was likely to be honed to a science. "A slick nigger," he said, "can steal a chicken out of a cooking pot and never take the lid off." Niggers came in all shades and colors, shapes and sizes, but were indiscriminate in their schedule of deficits whether they be black, yellow, old, kinky-headed, roguish, a buck or a preacher, a yard boy, a roustabout, bootlegger, Jack leg, hambone, or tater bug. Whatever else, he was still a nigger like God intended him to be, and that's all there was to that. *All niggers are the same, but they just got different styles.* God made them niggers, they made themselves whatever *kind* of niggers they turned out to be.

To be a good nigger was to be blessed with the active goodwill of the white folks, an asset of extraordinary importance, though it might on occasion incur the febrile disdain of some Blacks who in the privacy of the outhouse might manage a mumbled "Uncle Tom." But to be called a "good nigger" was a near-absolute guarantee against being mistreated by anybody, white or black. *Good niggers don't go hungry.* That was the critical lesson within a lesson. To be a good nigger meant that petty breaches of the law were overlooked or forgiven. It meant being looked after or provided for in sickness or distress. It meant having your credit or your credibility "stood for," and your funeral graced by the presence of white folks when you died.

In return for these rewards, the good nigger served faithfully and uncomplainingly at his appointed tasks in his appointed place. His wages were low, for he did not expect to be paid for his *work,* but for his *worth,* which was predetermined by other factors. He stayed out of trouble, minded his own business, and faithfully reported the business of other Negroes "downtown" as soon as he learned of it. He knew intuitively what was expected of him, and he did it. He knew his place, and he kept it. He might not be too bright, but according to Mr. Dubbie Gee, "God gave him motherwit to know it, so he ain't troubled and he ain't likely to trouble nobody else."

The bad nigger was not necessarily the antithesis of the good nigger. A bad nigger could have many of the characteristics of a good nigger and still be a bad nigger because the bad nigger's bad behavior was primarily confined to the black community, Black on Black. It was an in-group phenomenon of otherwise unacceptable behavior feeding on its own flesh. However, according to Mr. Martin, the "rambunctious" nature of the bad nigger occasionally became an intolerable annoyance for the white folks when his drinkin' and gamblin', cuttin' and shootin' and otherwise mean and unpredictable behavior became the principle cause of Monday morning absenteeism in the domestic workforce. When that happened often enough, Monday morning usually found the bad nigger in jail.

Now, it is paradoxical that in spite of the inconvenience he occasionally caused the white folks, there was apt to be a certain benignity, if not tacit approval, for the bad nigger, who could with selective endorsement be made to function as a convenient agent of control for others who might be tempted to stray out of place. Moreover, without the weekend exploits of the bad nigger, what would there be to titillate the conversation around Courthouse Square after the good nigger had made his Monday morning report?

Actually, the "bad nigger" in Mr. Martin's lexicon was called "half-bad" or "go-for-bad nigger" by other Blacks who were his peers. There was a true, or "sure-nuff," bad nigger who was a legend in every black community. This bad nigger "didn't take low" to *nobody,* black *or* white. And *nobody* laid a hand on him and lived, because he'd sooner die than let somebody break him to the saddle. Maybe that's why Mr. Dubbie Gee never talked about *him.* Maybe he was dead already.

It was the smart nigger that Mr. Martin considered the most unacceptable threat to the way things were supposed to be. The smart nigger was likely to be everything the good nigger was not. Most likely he was educated above the norm considered sufficient for colored folks; whether he got it in school or some bigger fool than he had put it into his head, he had some dangerous notions. In either case, Mr. Martin said that the smart nigger was a pain in his own ass, and everybody else's too. He wanted too much. He wanted his street paved, and he wanted it paved because he paid taxes rather than because his wife cooked for the judge. His house was painted and well kept and he didn't waste his money on rattletrap cars. He didn't "owe money downtown," or "take up" advances on his pay every Monday morning. More than likely he had "been up North," and he had a colored newspaper come to his house in the mail. The smart nigger paid his poll taxes, and he was mighty slow, it seemed to Mr. Dubbie Gee, to answer when somebody said "Boy!" He didn't think that the bad nigger was funny, or that the good nigger could be trusted. Clearly, every smart nigger would bear watching. "*They don't last long*," Mr. Martin said, and he "flat out had no use for them." He said that if *he* were colored he'd either kick a smart nigger's ass down off his shoulders or keep away from him. A smart nigger, he said "is a damn fool hell-bent for trouble. And mark my words, he's gon' find it quicker'n a catfish can suck a chicken gut off a bent pin."

By the time I was in high school I had internalized all the learnings I needed to cope with coming through the fire of race and place in Alabama. I knew the boundaries. There was a white world and a black world, and they were not the same. They touched or they abutted, occasionally they collided, and sometimes they overlapped, but they never merged. In Athens there was a college for girls, but not for the girls who graduated from my school. *They* went to work in the kitchens of the white folks. There was a park, but black kids could not play in it. It too was for whites only. There was a swimming pool. We were not allowed to use it—not even one day a week. We swam in the creek. So did the town's sewage. The railroad depot, the Greyhound bus station, the restrooms in the courthouse all had "White" and "Colored" signs. You couldn't sit at the counter in the five-and-ten-cent store to drink a Coke or eat a hotdog. If you went to the Ritz Theatre to see a western you had to enter through the alley and sit way, way upstairs in the gallery called "nigger heaven." The only place where black and white people could meet with any semblance of mutual dignity was at Trinity School, and this was possible only because there was a grudging, uncertain toleration of an enclave of Old Maid Yankees set on ruining the colored help with education they didn't understand and couldn't ever use. There was an occasion when even this tiny oasis of human civility would be challenged.

A visiting college choir was presenting a concert at Trinity. The principal invited "our white friends" from downtown to "come and share with us the rich experience" of that event as a gesture of goodwill and political cultivation. In compliance with local tradition, "special" seating in the auditorium was arranged for these white friends. To this I took exception, and as editor of the *Campus Chronicle* I denounced the overture as "an unconscionable desecration of the only island of probity in the whole state of Alabama." But islands of probity are not always sacrosanct, and when the faculty adviser to the paper refused to permit my editorial to be run, "the Three Charleses,"[2] as we were known thereafter by people less sensitive to such issues, went to press that night on our own. We mimeographed the forbidden article and plastered it around the campus and the adjacent community. The furor it created the next day had consequences somewhat larger than we had anticipated, and I lost my part-time job with some of the choicest language from Mr. Martin that southern biliousness could afford. It was an ungracious parting, but a timely one for me, for it was the first overt fracture of the symbols of my bondage. Thereafter, my days in Alabama would be numbered from one sunrise to the next.

NOTHING ON THE PROGRAM

There were six or eight black churches in Athens, almost all of them Methodist or Baptist. Grandma and I went to Village View Methodist, Reverend L. G. Fields, Pastor. Ma Matt was very proud of being a Methodist. It was one of the ways in which she punctuated her identity, and she paid twenty-five cents "dues" every week for the privilege. Often that quarter she kept knotted in the corner of her dress handkerchief was the only money there was in the house, but she never sacrificed it to personal exigence. It belonged to the Lord. Papa didn't have anything to do with the church. Everybody, black and white, said he was as good a man

2. William Charles Mason, Charles Wesley Tisdale, and Charles Eric Lincoln. Charles Mason was a casualty of World War II. Charles Tisdale publishes the bullet-scarred, award-winning *Jackson Advocate* in Jackson, Mississippi.

as you were likely to find in Alabama, but he just didn't have anything to do with the church. I guess I wondered why, but I never did ask anybody. I just went on with Ma Matt every Sunday the Lord sent, and sometimes on Wednesday night too. I felt secure in the church. God and Ma Matt were there.

The white churches were different, although I didn't know exactly why. I always wondered whether God was in them too, since Ma Matt was not. They seemed so imposing, so imperious. Maybe white churches didn't really need God. I wondered a lot about that. During the Christmas season of the last year I was to spend in Alabama, Charles Wesley Tisdale and I were walking in the downtown area in the vicinity of a large, awe-inspiring church. As we strolled along we could hear the magnificent crescendos of a pipe organ in tandem with what must have been a very large mass choir of mixed voices. It was the Hallelujah Chorus of Handel's *Messiah*. We stopped near the church to listen. Such music we had never heard before except on records or over the radio. Nor had either of us ever been close to a pipe organ. The music was so compelling that we permitted ourselves to be lost for a moment, enraptured by the magnificence of it all. But in that moment of spiritual ecstasy we wandered too close to the doors of the church. Suddenly we were thrust back into earthly reality by a white man who met us on the broad concrete steps outside the sanctuary. He was extremely agitated, although he must have known that we had no intention of trying to come into a white church. Panting and flushed with consternation, he cried out: "Get away from here! Get away from here! You niggers can't be standing on these steps! They'll be coming out of there any minute now, and there ain't a-going to be no niggers straggling around out here when they do!" Frantically, he waved us away from the church and into the street.

"Mister, we didn't mean no harm," I protested. "We just wanted to hear the organ and the singing."

"Boy, it don't make no difference what you want," he said. "Not one bit of difference. This here is a white church, and *There ain't nothing on the program for no niggers! Not a blessed thing!*" His flailing right arm etched an imaginary *X* on the air for emphasis.

"Nothing!" he repeated. "Now y'all git on back over yonder where you belong and don't be hanging 'round the doors of this church ever no more. Ain't a thing in there for you!"

As the deacon, or whatever he was, opened the ornate door to go back into the church, a final snatch of Handel wrenched through, but the music didn't seem to soar any more.

Alabama had taught me my final lesson in race and place: *There ain't nothing on the program for no niggers. Not a thing in the world!*

ALABAMA POSTSCRIPT

A few months later I left Alabama to see what the "program" was like in the rest of America. My hopes were high. Outside the South, I had heard it said, those beautiful words of Robert Burns—"A man's a man for a' that"—had real meaning. I headed for Chicago to experience it for myself.

I had scarcely installed myself in the Thirty-eighth Street YMCA on the Chicago South Side when I was invited by Dr. Jay T. Wright to spend a weekend with him in his parents' home in Green Bay, Wisconsin. Dr. Wright was the new headmaster at Trinity School, succeeding the venerable Louise H. Allyn, who had held that post for more than thirty years. Green Bay was to be my first real encounter with the world of white folks outside the state of Alabama. I looked forward to that new experience. But my initial encounter with that other world proved somewhat dismaying, or at least it got off to an unanticipated launching. Living next door to the Wrights was an Irish family that included a beautiful red-haired teenager about my own age, named Gloria. She came out to the backyard fence where Jay and I were enjoying a game of catch.

"Hi!" she said extending her hand across the palings. "My name is Gloria. What's yours? Would you please smile so that I can see your pretty white teeth? Tell me, why do the Negro people in the South carry razors and eat—what is it, 'possums all the time? I've never been to the South except to Chicago, but I don't think I'd like to live there. It's a dreadful place, don't you think? I hope you'll stay up here where it's nice." Just then, I didn't know quite *what* to hope.

After that introduction to Green Bay, on the following day Jay and I drove to Appleton, Wisconsin, to visit his married sister. On the way Jay told me a little about Appleton: It was the home of Senator Joe McCarthy, the dubious scourge of crypto-communism, he said. And no colored people lived there as far as he knew. Well, perhaps not, but I was soon to find out that whether they lived there or not, there was a structure in place for dealing with them. I was given the guest bedroom at Jay's sister's house, and when I awoke the next morning I was vaguely aware that I was not alone. As a matter of fact, I had apparently been sleeping before an extensive audience of curious little urchins from all over the neighborhood. For how long, I had no way of knowing, but when I opened my eyes my incredulous blinks met the steady stares of Barbara, aged six, and seven or eight of her playmates. Barbara was the daughter of my hosts, and on this particular morning she was surely the unchallenged impresario of the neighborhood. There was a show going on, and I was Exhibit 1.

"You see there?" Barbara was saying as my consciousness caught up with my vision. "You see there? I told you we had a brown man at our house, and there he is, *right there!*" The motley passel of little urchins edged a bit closer and peered more intently. "My Uncle Jay brought him from Chicago," Barbara declared, "and he's ours. We're going to keep him *right here!* Now go on and say 'Good morning' to him. My mother says you have to do it."

One by one several of the timid little company trotted by the bed mouthing a muffled "Goo' Morning, Brown Man!" and so on out the door to less stressful encounters. That is, until one little blue-eyed, towheaded maverick ambled up to the bedside, planted his feet, and pointed an accusatory finger: "That," he declared pontifically, "ain't neither no 'brown man.' That there ain't nothing but a great big ole nigger, and *don't nobody have to say nothing to him!*" With that, he stuck out his tongue at me in gleeful derision, made a "whooshing" noise, waved his fingers in his ears, and pattered on out of my bedroom. There was a look of triumph on his cherubic-impish countenance, but my hopes for a place on "the program" "up north" were already lying shattered at the foot of my borrowed bed. *Don't nobody have to say nothing to a nigger.* A nigger is a nonentity by definition. Damn! I turned over and tried to go back to sleep. I had to come all the way to Wisconsin to find out what I had already learned in Alabama.

Five months later—Sunday, December 7, 1941, it was, I rounded up my little clutch of buddies at the Thirty-eighth Street "Y" and we all went to the naval recruiting office in downtown Chicago to join the U.S. Navy. Pearl Harbor had been attacked, and we were at war. There were seven of us, mostly from the South, and one or two underage, but all of us ready to fight and die for our country.

The salty old bosun's mate handling the recruiting traffic turned us aside at the door, shaking his grizzled old head and waving his hash marks and sounding very much like he was reading from a script: "You boys g'won back home," he said. "We ain't taking no niggers in the Navy today. Just fightin' men." *No niggers, just fightin' men!* That's what he said. He then waved a group of white boys forward, signifying that our interview was concluded. "You men get on up there to the counter and sign up," he said to the white volunteers. "Step lively now, we got to go kill ourselves some Japs!"

The war went on, and in due course I received an official-looking letter from the president of the United States. "Greetings!" it said. The next thing I knew I was a "fightin' man" in a navy uniform, but I hadn't changed my color to any perceptible degree. The president said that we were fighting for four freedoms: Freedom from Fear, Freedom from Want, Freedom of Religion, and Freedom of Conscience. I wished that he had added a fifth freedom—Freedom from the *Fire* I mistakenly thought I had left behind me in Alabama when I made it to Chicago. But those were the salad days of my innocence, and little did I dream that it would take considerably more than a global war for four massive freedoms abroad to establish one small freedom at home.

III

MIND AND COUNTERMIND: RACE AND PLACE IN CONTEXT

O Land

Land of the free

Home of the brave

Will ever there be

For the Son of a slave

A place in your scheme

The American Dream?

—C. ERIC LINCOLN,

This Road since Freedom

Race is a matter of mind. It has no objective reality. Yet, in what we like to believe is the most enlightened civilization on earth, the pollution of the national mentality by the fantasies of social preemption demonstrates the tenacity with which we cling to the primitive urges of our moral and intellectual infancy. It is all a matter of mind, but the mind-sets we institutionalize as values inevitably set the stage for the fear and alienation that fracture the society and torture us all with a pervasive sense of contradiction. It is all a matter of mind, but too often the mind wavers and shrinks in uncertainty in the confrontation with the ever-hovering specter of antimind.

MIND AND COUNTERMIND

I used to spend a lot of time thinking about race. It just didn't make sense to me. Too many contradictions. Too many nonsequiturs. Too illogical. Too mechanical. Too humanistically sterile.

In one of the quiet places I used to go to be alone with my thoughts there was a small reproduction of Rodin's magnificent sculpture *The Thinker.* It is an irenic figure, somehow managing to capture, among other things, what I like to call "the serenity of cerebration," a kind of joyful peace that comes with the realization that something exciting is happening in the mind. Perhaps Rodin had solved the riddle of race, and that was what gave his sculpture the pervasive sense of peace that it seemed to exude. At such times I realized all over again that thinking is an intrinsic value—a value in and of itself. Human beings are meant to think, and when they fail to do so, not only do they expose themselves to the consequences of ignorance and inanity, they also deprive themselves of one of the most rewarding experiences available to the human spectrum of possibility—the organization and creative management of ideas in the ongoing search for reality.

But thinking can be painful. Thinking has its risks and its hazards. Chimeras come unbidden into the mind and lodge themselves in the remote interstices of recollection. Besides, our culture has often been ambivalent about its thinkers. Scientists and men and women of letters from Copernicus to W. E. B. Du Bois have from time to time stirred the suspicion and suffered the hostility of contemporaries who felt threatened by having in their midst anyone committed to the purification of ideas. Book burning as a feature of our past intellectual phobias has its contemporary counterpart in book banning, selective publication, and political correctness—which is to say public consensus under duress. Group-think has always been the "safest" expression of cerebration, if there is one, and even today people are no more comfortable with independent thinking than they were when Columbus acted out his novel geographical theorem by sailing west in his efforts to reach the East. The common turn of mind remains the sine qua non of the common code of acceptance, and from this remarkable non sequitur derive the endless minutiae addressed to the validation and the substantiation of what has already been determined by common consent.

On the other hand, to our great credit in American academe we regularly interrupt the circuitry of an otherwise closed system of thinking by creating islands of intellectual independence somewhat beyond the tidewaters of the main. At the national level, we endow the arts and humanities and the sciences with limited financial resources designed for the support of a variety of expressions of independent thought. We endow chairs in the universities and award prestigious prizes, medals, titles, and other emoluments to those whose thinking turns out to be of unusual benefit to humankind or opens new frontiers of learning. Independent thinkers remain suspect as a class, but there is a certain pragmatism in our ambivalence which permits them, however much we begrudge it, to keep on thinking lest the public interest be irretrievably compromised. Perhaps deep in our cultural subconsciousness there is a covert hope that sooner or later some thinker will think of a way to make thinking fail-safe, or that in time thinking may even become obsolete, thus solving its own problem. In the meantime, we need to address our best thinking to one of our most persistent problems. We need to think about race and the implications of race which have crippled and maimed our society for about four hundred years and are now threatening its untimely dissolution.

It is at this point that the anomaly of our great universities takes on peculiar significance, for the university, properly conceived, exists as a midwife for the delivery of ideas. The university is the ultimate stage for the pursuit of truth, and truth unadorned is the goal of all serious thinking. The true university initiates and endows *the great conversation,* the exchange of ideas to be tried and tested in the crucible of contrariety. It is a place where no dogma is sacred except the dogma that rejects all dogmas, but where the recognition of the right to question, to challenge, and to disagree is itself the clearest index of the commitment to reason this society is likely to produce. In the true university, the optimum possibilities of the intellectual enterprise are promoted when earnest scholars at varying levels of maturation attend each other in the interest of the total society they exist to serve. Some may be called professors, others may be called students, but their common task is to exchange ideas, to test the quality of ideas, and to examine and refine the processes through which improved ideas may come into being, be communicated, and find their proper expression in the enhancement of the human condition. In short, the university exists for the celebration and the instrumentation of learning, and learning is the principal means through which a society sustains itself, renews itself, and validates its continued existence. Nevertheless, there is reason to doubt whether the enormous investment underpinning institutionalized learning in the United States has significantly reduced our most pressing cultural deficits in the last one hundred years.

Thinking is the precondition of learning, and learning unsupported by thinking is mere rote conditioning, or learning in a state of paralysis. That is why institutions of learning grow stale and lose their significance when intellectual ferment fizzles and dies. If there is nothing being thought, there is nothing of significance being taught, and the academic conversation becomes trivial, puerile, and inconsequential. The mere mixing of students and professors in the same space does not guarantee that any learning is dispensed, or that any learning takes place. Time was when our institutions of higher learning were deliberately isolated from the common people, but this was in the days when the objectives and function of learning were less clearly understood, and when the college or university considered itself an intellectual "asylum." We have long since learned that such institutions must either import reality in the form of issues or problems of human existence, accept irrelevance, or die. Real life is the critical datum of instruction. It is also the catalyst which stirs the continuing debate that is the mother of the very ideas addressed to its understanding. In consequence, the college or university which exists merely as a retreat for the privileged is a genteel anachronism, unworthy of the public trust and support. It serves no purpose of consequence. Its thinking professors soon think their way to more exciting appointments on other campuses, and thinking students prove it by not going there in the first place. Nevertheless, the critical problems of race and place which wrack this society are still not prominent among the critical interests of the intellectual enterprise. Dare we wonder why?

Ever since René Descartes offered the intriguing postulate *cogito ergo sum,* there have been those who have taken unwarranted comfort in the confused notion that mere existence is the evidence of cerebration. Not so. To be is not necessarily to be thinking, and we do not like to think about problems that defy solution. Thinking implies, at a minimum, effort, end, and motivation. Hence, there are those who find thinking a chore or an unnecessary deferment of more important interests they wish to pursue. It is said that Emperor Franz Joseph of Austria, for example, when pressed with an annoying problem of state, routinely promised to "have it thought about." He then assigned the thinking to others so that his own mind could be free to pursue the elaborate pomp and pageantry of the court. The point I am making is that although the capacity to think is a human attribute synonymous with existence, the exercise of that capacity involves both will and effort, and the quality of the effort is bound to be reflected in the end result.

Thinking about race and place is a form of inquiry, and all serious inquiry aims at the discovery of truth or the understanding of reality. An old legend illustrates the problems inherent in the pursuit of truth and knowledge. It seems that one day when some of the gods were disporting themselves atop Mount Olympus, they inadvertently dislodged the Jewel of Truth from its setting in the royal diadem. Before anyone could recover it, Truth tumbled down the side of the mountain and splintered into a million fragments on the rocks below. Scrambling about in consummate ignorance in the darkness at the foot of Olympus, man chanced to spy one of the fragments. Clutching it to his breast he exclaimed: "Look! Look! I have found the truth! Now I shall be like the gods!"

Perhaps. But a fragment of truth hardly makes one an Olympian, and even the most able and prestigious scrambler among us holds but a fragment of the jewel, and not the Jewel of Truth itself. In a world looking for the quick fix and the instant answer, the maximization of fragmentation functions to endow with inordinate value selected fragments of truth which are then made to answer for all the truth that is missing. Such sophistry may have a compelling allure, but to yield to it is to close the book prematurely—before all the data are in. The truth about race is certainly not all in. Perhaps a more responsible commitment to the quality of thinking than we have shown a willingness to indulge may in time produce the larger truths we need to see us for what we are rather than what our errant egos would have us believe. When the self sits in judgment of its own credibility, any verdict it may render ought to be taken with a liberal dash of salt. We should be both encouraged and sobered by the realization that for all our present learning, we have seen only the nip of the tip of the berg of reality, and that indistinctly. Nor do we seem to be close to understanding the integrality or the full meaning of what we do see, for if we did, the pervasive specter of race and place which stalks our civilization and poisons our most intimate relationships would long since have been banished from the roster of problems that press us for resolution.

In America, *race* is the touchstone of all value, the prism through which all else of significance must be refracted before relationships can be defined or relevance ascertained. There is no order of reality large enough to transcend its pervasiveness, small enough to escape its intrusiveness, or independent enough to avoid its imprimatur. In the colleges and universities, where the quality of thinking is the alleged measure of intellectual distinction, all true distinctiveness is blurred by the pallor of a common worldview which begins with the presumptions of fantasy, and not the lucidity of reason. Such thinking is not true thinking at all, but merely the flexing of the muscles of cultural fatuity. The great conversation is demeaned, and the stuff of learning is reduced to the pap of a sanitized, coercive collegiality. Such "political correctness" lacks the security of minds that can agree to disagree and still remain in community until a larger truth emerges from the hazy surrealistic afterglow that is made to pass for luminescence.

Truth has a moral dimension that provides the integrative tension by means of which all of the fragments of human experience are held in proper juxtaposition, making possible a more perfect scenario of who we are, and why. Thinking effectively implies a worldview—a comprehensive perspective—informed by an ethic, by means of which some pattern of reason within the chaos with which we struggle is discernible. It is to this end that our best thinking must be addressed. We have pulverized the atom, but we seem to have no clear notion of why, except because it was there. We have walked on the moon, but we see no relation between that feat and the fact that we have not yet learned to walk peaceably with each other here on earth. We have unlocked the innermost secrets of genetic composition, but if we have learned anything about the sacredness of human life, it is not revealed in the statistics that illustrate our mania for its abuse and destruction. In our redoubtable impudence, we reach for the stars across the fathomless expanses of space, but we do not reach for each other across the fictitious chasms of race. We can do better, and we must do better or forfeit for all time that precious spark of divine endowment that makes us uniquely human.

The times we live in certainly require more than a casual approach to the business of thinking straight. Our problems are massive, and we live with perpetual anxiety; but our possibilities are as viable as our efforts to realize them. Neither the catharsis of overkill nor the narcosis of avoidance can ever be an effective substitute for thinking things through. Indeed, the senseless bang and the graceless whimper are alike demeaning in a society so generously endowed to excel. *We can think. We can reason. We can be better than we are.*

To see life steadily and to see it whole; to know, and to make knowing an instrument of freedom and creativity; to understand the stars without reducing them to pollution; to appreciate love without being maudlin in its expression; to care about the nurturing green earth, and to nurture it in turn; and above all, to recognize that human contingency is but the counterpart of human interdependency—that is our challenge. We are all a part of the main. The erosion that crumbles the common shoreline feeds on the stuff of the whole that is our point of departure.

THE AMERICAN DILEMMA

The United States as a nation has preferred not to think too deeply about its racial problems, and unlike Franz Joseph of Austria, has rarely appointed anyone else to do the thinking our responsible intellectual and political leadership has consistently failed to do. In our early history as a nation we chose to be flattered by the observations of Alexis de Tocqueville, the distinguished French scholar who traversed our young nation and carefully noted the probable sources from which problems would be likely to arise in the future; race was prominent among them. But aside from the charm of his manners and the cut of his clothes, we did not take de Tocqueville very seriously. A century or so later, on the eve of World War II, we brought in Gunnar Myrdal to actually research our racial problems and give us his prognosis for the future. After several years of gathering data and testing some hypotheses based on presuppositions that proved to be distressingly familiar, Dr. Myrdal nevertheless conceded that America had a "dilemma." It was a *moral* dilemma issuing from the vast gap between America's self-image as a Christian culture and America's actual behavior that sorely strained that characterization. During the waning days of the civil rights revolution which wracked our society for more than a generation following the end of the last world war, the Kerner Commission, a high-level investigative task force appointed by President Lyndon Johnson and headed by Theodore Hesburgh, president of Notre Dame University, revealed in their "Kerner Report" the somber findings that America was in fact *two* societies: one white and one black, separate and unequal, and featuring racism as the principal fodder by which our two-headed buffalo is nourished and sustained.

Serious self-study is not the typical means by which we come to know what we know, or claim to know, about the pervasiveness of racism. Reliable scholarly research and serious official studies are relatively rare given the enormity of the problem. Instead we get our chief "information" by the winnowing of selective experience, both personal and vicarious. Inevitably, unbiased perception is blocked by the unending chain of impressions we internalize as "experience" when no true objective experience has taken place. These impressions become the principal signposts of what we do not know rather than reliable projections of reality distilled from critical thinking and open-minded observation.

The media are the principal source of distilled vicarious "information." But such information may well be tainted with special interests or polluted with irrelevance. Entertainment and information are not necessarily the same; nor does a printed version of conventional wisdom enhance its credibility. The press sees what it is equipped to see, and the critical component of that equipment is the human agent through whose perceptions "the truth" (*the whole truth?*) is refracted. In the long, news-flat dog days of the slow-moving summer of the arrest of black O. J. Simpson for the murder of his white ex-wife, the news media reached the nadir of irresponsibility. So scandalous was the "professional" behavior of the media that the judge hearing the case felt compelled to suspend the jury selection process, and the question of whether Mr. Simpson could get a fair trial anywhere in America began to threaten seriously the public confidence in our system of justice. That question will probably tug at the drawstrings of the American conscience long after the O. J. Simpson trial is history. The larger question, however, is how *anyone* of whatever race can be assured of justice in a society in which race is so vital a determinant in the way people "see" and respond to what they see.

THE MIND OF THE SOUTH

My personal feelings about the limitations of the journalistic enterprise as a reliable index of the critical aspects of our racial dilemma were institutionalized quite early. It happened about the same time I learned that the fire of race and place was not a local phenomenon endemic to a class of mean-spirited people in Alabama, but that "the South" was everywhere people made race a frontier of personal confrontation or a pretext for the differential treatment of selected others unable to register their objections with effective deterrence. I mark that new consciousness with the reading of a book, *The Mind of the South,* written by W. G. Cash and published in 1941. Ironically, I didn't have to read Mr. Cash's book to find out about the southern turn of mind on the eve of World War II. I was of the South and in the South experiencing the ruminations of that mind firsthand. At the time his book was published "Jack" Cash was a working journalist in Chicago. He had migrated there from his native Gaffney, South Carolina, and his clever revelations caused a substantial ripple of excitement and titillation among the circles of northern and eastern literati who were always on the alert for a new Thomas Wolfe, or a William Faulkner, or perhaps even a new Thomas Dixon to rise up out of the South to entertain them with the charming drollery of that region. "Penetrating and persuasive," wrote the *New York Times* of *The Mind of the South.* Unflappable *Time* magazine was even more effusive, deciding that "anyone writing about the South henceforth must start where he leaves off." Perhaps. But if that were to be the case, we would forfeit some intriguing nuances of southern mind that Jack Cash, for all his candor and cleverness, may have overlooked. After all, he was only forty-one years old when his book came off the press, and as fate would have it, there would be little time left him for reconsideration; he died within a year. In any case, while Cash's perspectives were engagingly articulated, they were hardly unique; and while *The Mind of the South* is a convenient point of reference, it is the functioning mind of the South as the counterpart of the mind of America that excites my response, long after I left the South thoroughly confused by what I experienced there.

Nineteen forty-one marked a critical point of redefinition in my life. It was the year I became a man, consciously responsible for my own survival, and for the consequences of my own decisions. My first decision as a man had been to leave Alabama—to get out of the fire. To be free. To be a man among men, not just a counterfeit man commonly called a nigger and assigned to the dung patrol of a civilization from which I was functionally excluded. Chicago was to be the symbol of my liberation, my coming of age—the chrysalis of my manhood. That was my fantasy. But Chicago was not remotely prepared, and cared even less, for who I thought I was, or who I wanted to be. And there was Jack Cash, lately of South Carolina, who had preempted the mind of Chicago with a dubious narration designed to cut the ground from under me as a "Negro" from the South by leaving me out of mind and capable of nothing beyond "singing sad songs in the cotton." I never met W. J. Cash, of course, but at that stage of my life I regarded him and his work as a personal affront to black people in general and to my own sense of identity in particular. My youthful insouciance probably never quite forgave Mr. Cash, although I have recognized long since that my reception in Chicago and elsewhere in America was hardly due to his spreading the word about the southern mind just at the moment I thought I was crossing the Jordan. A half century has passed, yet Cash's work remains a useful backdrop against which to measure today's mind of the South as a reliable index to the mind of America.

The South, according to Cash, is that area of America "roughly delineated by the boundaries of the former Confederate States . . . shading over into some . . . border states . . . [and exhibiting] a fairly definite mental pattern, associated with a fairly definite social pattern [and] a complex of established relationships and habits of thought, sentiments, prejudices, standards and values." Hence the South, as Cash understands it, is a state of mind geographically defined: a kind of regional Weltanschauung that could not exist in the absence of any of its principals. The definition is clear enough, but its utility is seriously emasculated when the principals, as Cash perceives them, are so delimited as to exclude for all practical purposes the one component that makes sense of all the others. Cash's mind of the South is a mind strictly limited by race. It is a *white* mind—in Cash's terms, a "superior mind" of the "best people"—to which has been ceded custody, care, and articulation of whatever sentiments and values lower-class whites may once have claimed for themselves. Black southerners were, it seems, "out of mind" altogether, and because they were, the limitations of Cash's excursus begin at the beginning and persist throughout his book. I could have told Jack Cash that the South was, and is, about *black* people, people he knew on his best behavior as "Negroes." We call them African Americans today, and they figure with implacable pervasiveness in every identifiable interest by which that region was, and will be, defined: economics, law, jurisprudence, politics, religion, sex, social relations—the list is endless. Take away the black component and the whole notion of "the South" collapses. It becomes unimaginable, like Lawrence of Arabia with no Arabs. It is patent, of course, that Cash's "mind of the South" has no black component, not because there were no black people there but because in the prevailing order of race and place the black mind had no voice and was in consequence inconsequential. This is a specious argument: a blunderous misperception, for however suppressed and however unavailable it may have been to white insensitivity and ridicule, there was indeed a black mentality. History will confirm that far from being asleep among the cotton rows, and despite being officially denied and publicly ignored, the cerebrations of that mentality seeped into the ruling white mind extolled by Cash and left an understated impress there. In time, that unrecognized deposit of human affirmation would be called on to help the South through the trauma of transition. Cash's decision to go with convention, extolling the "ancient docility" of the Africans in America, left him supinely vulnerable to the questions of a larger, less indulgent reality than the one he wrote about.

I know something about the mind of the South. I was in the South and of the South the same time W. J. Cash was there participating in that "mind" on which he would later unshutter the windows of the big house and give the world a qualified look. Cash was writing about the South projected by the "best white men," by the ruling hegemony. I was a part of the South, Cash's South, but by Cash's definition I was not a part of the southern mind. Nor could I ever be. But I was a part of what that mindset was all about; and being black, I was the definitive focus of that mind, its raison d'être. Leave me out, and "the South" did not, does not, will not exist, and W. J. Cash's daring and intriguing sociological apology self-destructs for want of substance, for want of reason, for want of opportunity. It is mere sound and fury, significant, perhaps, of nothing more serious than "the Southern fondness for rhetoric" to which he laid claim as his heritage. Still, it must be recognized that the most engaging rhetorical romance is not necessarily reliable sociology. No commentary on Yoknapatawpha could be seriously considered which excluded "Negroes" as a prime ingredient of its ambience, and W. J. Cash's more ambitious excursus is no exception. The black presence is indeed a part of an unstated premise by which his book is informed, but it is so subdued as to render that presence an innocuous human tapestry depicting "sad songs in the cotton."

I was born in Alabama and I grew up in Alabama, and if that does not entitle me to membership or participation in the mind of the South, it at least gives reasonable certification to my credentials for commenting on that mind. I am, in Langston Hughes's words, the "darker brother," but to borrow a different imagery from T. S. Eliot, I am also, in Cash's "mind," "form without substance, paralysed force."[1] But I do exist, and thanks to the generosity of Cartesian logic, it is probable that I also think, although I concede in advance that mere thinking is not necessarily thinking relevantly. Relevance, alas! is a determination to be made after the egg has been laid, a common exposure to the rigors of reason and

1. Adapted from T. S. Eliot, "The Hollow Men" (1925), in Eliot, *The Complete Poems and Plays* (New York: Harcourt Brace, 1952), p. 56.

the rantings of fools and politicians alike. Be that as it may, it is mine to insist that I am a real live thinking human being, and that the principal struggles of my life are the objective affirmations of that fact, whatever the final determinations of others may be.

The year *The Mind of the South* was published was the year I dated my emancipation from that mind. I left Alabama in 1941 and headed north to Chicago. I wrote on the lid of the shoe-box I carried stuffed with fried chicken, two-egg cornbread, a roasted sweet potato, and Grandma's prayers the sentiments that compelled my departure:

> Thou art my native state
> But am I proud?
> My being seethes with hate
> And like a cloud
> Cruel scenes flock back to me
> Of greed and death
> Of fear and misery
> Here's to your health.[2]

I was leaving Alabama; I was leaving the South. But how could I have known that I was not necessarily leaving the mind of the South? Having come out of the South a little earlier, Cash had already discovered what I was hardly prepared to learn—that the mind of the South "proceeds from the common American heritage, and many of its elements are readily recognizable as simply variations on the primary American theme." I had judged Alabama in the fitful flare of a miner's lamp struggling against the stygian darkness of that nether world that was the South for anyone of African descent. When I had seen a whole lot more of America and my "native state" came to encompass that larger universe, I would call back that earlier judgment for modification in the light of a broadened experience sobered by a new set of realities I had not yet encountered when I escaped to the vaunted freedom of the North.

2. "Toast to My Native State" (unpublished manuscript by C. Eric Lincoln).

EXPERIENCING "THE MIND"

I know experientially what Cash was writing about. I know about "black men singing . . . sad songs in the cotton." I know because I was there in the cotton, and I was black. And if I never sang sad songs on such occasions, I heard those who did and cursed them for their resignation. And if I didn't know that the "po' crackers" and the "white trash" Cash refers to as that "vague race lumped together indiscriminately" sprang "for the most part from convict servants, redemptioners, and debtors," I did know instinctively to stay away from them. Whatever their origins, po' white trash meant trouble—lots of trouble. And to many a black man that trouble proved terminal. Growing up in the South, I learned about that at about the same time I learned my name. But that instinct was constantly reinforced by precept and by inculcation—every day—so dread were the consequences of not knowing. Long before I reached puberty my grandmother was constant and insistent: "Don't have nothing to do with that trash hanging around the courthouse yard. Don't fight with them redneck boys, and don't look at them po' white gals." If her message was cryptic, its meaning was clear and unmistakable: Don't give the rednecks, the crackers, the po' white trash any pretext to hang you from a tree or roast you on some muddy creekbank. It was a reasonably effective prescription for surviving Jack Cash's mind of the South.

I was in the South. I was one of those boys with a sprinkling of hair on his lip and a voice that alternately rumbled and quavered. And if my life circumstances required that I venture with regularity into the forbidden valley among forbidding people, then my survival depended on how innocuously invisible I could make myself until my fateful foray could be accomplished. Yes, I knew the po' white trash had an unabated lust for my discomfiture and for my blood, that they represented an unrelenting commitment to my nonbeing. At the time, I didn't understand why. It didn't make sense to me. Nor did I know that behind the so-called rednecks who so readily laid down their Bibles, quit their revivals, and leaped from their pulpits to go "coon huntin'," was all the time the stealthy hand of the "quality white folk" who taught the blacks to hate the "white trash" in the first place. Mr. Cash calls these "the best people," and it was not until he laid bare the controlling mind of the South in contrast to the reactive impulses of his "common man" that the vision of quality so carefully nurtured in the big house and its derivative institutions began to fade and drip.

I worked for "quality folks" for fifty cents a week and my breakfast, leaving home at three in the morning to be "milk boy" for a small dairy. I washed the steel crates of thick, heavy glass bottles and delivered the milk and cream to the front porches of the sleeping gentry until eight in the morning. Every morning. Grandpa milked eighteen cows twice a day. Every day. For that the "best people" paid him $3.50 a week and praised him for his industry. Grandma washed and ironed for the same family of five white folks of the very best quality, including two elderly spinster ladies whose crinolines and ruffles and pleated shirtwaists kept her busy "rubbing" in a tin tub on our back porch and "pressing" with a pair of sadirons heated in the fireplace from Monday to Saturday. Every week. Winter and summer. For this, the "best people" paid her $1.25 and called her "A'nt Mattie" with the peculiar affection and respect quality white folks reserve for their favorite black retainers.

That $5.25 we managed to eke out together, augmented by an additional thirty-five cents I got in the summertime for watering the flowers and mowing the lawn for another quality family, meant survival. It was also the wages of accommodation to a system that taught us to work without stinting, hate the cracker, be suspicious of the Jew, and maintain a developed sense of contingency to a recognized family of the ruling class. This was the understanding that put bread and salt pork and a jar of blackstrap molasses on the table of the "good"—that is, the accommodated—Negroes; insured them against "trouble with the law"; kept the po' white trash at bay; sent the white doctor to see them when they were down sick; and graced their funerals with a benign white presence when they died.

Despite the official posture of hostility and the perceived sacred mission to keep the nigger in his place, elements of Cash's "common whites," including po' white trash, on occasion (covert though it had to be) carried on relationships with black people, which except for the cultural stigma against such a thing would have been called "friendships." They fished and hunted with Blacks, drank rotgut whiskey with Blacks, and not infrequently ate and slept with Blacks. I was there, and I knew such people and such relationships. Black midwives often "pulled their young 'uns," and if color was in conflict with convention, some black mama took on another child she didn't birth to raise as her own. But such covert relationships were unreliable. The same faces sometimes seen in black cabins by day were just as likely to come back again at night ensconced in bedsheets and dunce caps, and lusting this time for blood. This was the official role of that class dictated by the conventions set by the best minds.

SOURCES OF COUNTERMIND

I know about the schools for Negroes Cash talks about. I know firsthand about the South's tardy takeover of the schools for the primary reason of ousting the Yankee schoolmarms from their lairs of black contamination. North Carolina's Charles Brantley Aycock's perception of "Yankee money and Yankee teachers . . . pouring down" and "plainly determined" on educating the Negroes was not without substance. In 1866 the American Missionary Association built a school for freedmen in Limestone County, north Alabama. It was promptly burned by the Ku Kluxers, but the Yankee zeal to bring enlightenment to the hapless victims of the South's "peculiar institution" was not to be trampled or discouraged by such arrant intimidation. They built it back. I am glad they did, for if they had not, there would have been no possibility of a high school education for me in my hometown of Athens when I was ready for that venture three quarters of a century later. High schools were there for the white children, but no public schools went beyond the sixth grade for blacks in my town and county until 1942, a year after the mind of the South had gone public through the literary efforts of a native son from Gaffney, South Carolina.

In a very curious way I benefited by that remission. In Athens, at Trinity School, I was safely in the hands of the "outsiders" from Boston, New London, New Haven, and other citadels of Yankee determination, while my friends and counterparts "out in the country" were treated by the state of Alabama to five to seven months of "schooling" each school year in one-room shacks with cardboard blackboards, no electricity, and outdoor "closets." In the winter these schools were heated by wood brought by the students and the teacher (who was privileged to work for thirty dollars a month); and when cotton-chopping time arrived in late March, and cotton-picking time extended from August into late October or early November, the schools were closed and the black children sent to the fields.

But at Trinity I was fortunate enough to receive the best education available in the area, provided by dedicated New England spinsters who did not teach for money, but who bargained away their lives and their comfort out of a sense of *ought* that the "best people" of the South were unable to entertain. Even Henry Grady's self-interest arguments, which prescribed limited training for the Negro that would "rigidly veto the ideas of academic schools for him," but would provide him the elementals of useful labor and inure him against raping white women, failed to garner any enthusiasm.

Nevertheless, there clearly was a problem, and it had to be dealt with—and soon. The misguided Christian errantry of the ever-meddlesome Yankee missionaries had already loosed upon the South a potentially dangerous horde of benighted Africans, who, now deprived of the resolute guidance of their God-appointed "masters," were already slopping hungrily at the proliferating troughs of exported Yankee education. Such a prospect was patently unacceptable to the distressed prevailing southern mind. The effective answer, reasoned Charles Brantley Aycock, was to defang the threat of the Yankee education of Negroes by having the South itself do the educating. Eventually, Aycock's logic found grudging and limited implementation, but his covert hope of truly meaningful education for Negroes was not to be.

Nevertheless, there had been a significant crack in the holding pens of ignorance. The African mind had been "discovered" and recognized. It was there and functioning in the South, despite all constraints. I was a case in point. At Trinity I read everything the library could afford and everything my delighted Yankee schoolmarms could import for me—Walter Scott, Shakespeare, Dryden, Pope, Goethe, Ovid, Pushkin, Plutarch, Milton, Plato, Aesop, Washington Irving, and the Transcendentalists. I also read the entire Bible at least three times. And in one of the barrels of clothing, books, and other reusables sent down from the North to be distributed at the school, I found the works of Karl Marx, Lenin, and Adam Smith, and read them inter alia with H. G. Wells, Kafka, Victor Hugo, Dostoyevski, Tolstoy, John Dewey, Richard Wright, and all the poets of the Harlem Renaissance. Twice a week (and any other time I could cadge the key to the school music room) I sat enraptured in another world listening to the music that poured out of the wind-up Victrola that stood gleaming majestically in mahogany and brass, waiting to share the wondrous works of Wagner, Beethoven, Schubert, Verdi, Bach, Strauss, Brahms, Rachmaninoff, and the Fisk Jubilee Singers. Certainly my opportunities were not typical, for none of this would have been remotely possible in any school or academic program the South provided for its black children. But thinking *was* going on among black people at whatever levels of opportunity and experience circumstances happened to permit, and that thinking was destined to become a countermind to the mind Cash recognized as the only significant expression of the southern perception of reality—past, present, and to come.

In 1942, a year after I quit Alabama for Chicago, the South's takeover program for Yankee-based Negro schools finally took over Trinity, and Camelot ceased to exist in north Alabama, just as it was being choked to death all across the South. Dr. Jay T. Wright, the last white principal at Trinity, was sent packing; the venerable New England teachers who had come out of Mount Holyoke eons before with the gleam of enlightenment in their eyes and the dream of Christian service in their hearts went back at last to limp out their remaining days among their ancestral Yankee roots.

All left save one, a Miss Mildred ——, who was not a Yankee

but a scion of one of Alabama's most prominent cotton-rich families, who as a young woman had offered herself as a teacher at Trinity. She was accepted, although with much fear and trembling for all concerned, and she was promptly disinherited by her family, who thereafter refused all communication with her. The price she paid for her commitment to Christian service, or whatever her private motivations may have been, can only be guessed at. Nobody seems to remember what happened to her after the dream ended and the denouement began. But the seeds of an alternative worldview of what the South was and what the South should become had already been sown, and not just by the Yankees. The South has always had an independent black mind, and the best evidence of its quality was its prudence of expression in the face of a consummate self-defeating futility. But time harbors a certain benevolence for patience and restraint.

In the place of the Yankee schoolmarms came "colored" teachers, native-born and educated in the ways and wiles of the South. It was not unusual for such faculties to have a local preacher at their head, adept at divining the mind of the South and putting that mind at ease. But the handwriting of things to come was even then on the wall, and in scarcely more than a decade the South's plan for Negro education would be shaken to its implausible foundations by the impossible demands brought on by *Brown v. Board of Education*. But the *Brown* case had long been in the making in that other mind Jack Cash had chosen to ignore. Now that mind was in the courts, challenging the dogma of convention and bent on reformulating the functioning southern temper forever. If a mind is a "terrible thing to waste," it can also be a perilous thing to ignore.

COMMUNISM

The southern preoccupation with communism was an aspect of the mind of the South that I rarely encountered while growing up in Alabama. My stumbling upon Marx and Lenin in the charity barrel at Trinity was fortuitous and not a part, I am sure, of any dark, Machiavellian Yankee attempt at secret indoctrination. Certainly there was never any discussion, or even any mention, of communism by any of my teachers. I read communist ideology with the same dispassionate innocence of intellectual inquiry as I read Thomas Jefferson and Cotton Mather. The cotton mills in my town had been closed, I guess, before I was born. They were still standing there, stark red brick surrounded by iron fences, but they were closed, and the whites who lived in the old mill houses were not likely to offer any explanations, even if they had any. The quality white folks were no more forthcoming, at least in my presence, so there was only the vague and shadowy legend that the mills were somehow connected with "Jews" who didn't live in Athens. The whole matter fell into the forbidden category of "white folks' business," which meant that blacks folks were to "let it alone."

About the only time I heard the word *communist* in Athens was in connection with the Scottsboro Boys. Scottsboro was only thirty or forty miles from where I grew up, so the case was much on the minds and in the covert conversations of black people I knew. The stately old mansion of the venerable Judge James E. Horton, who tried the case, was on my milk route, and I passed through his yard every day. The official wisdom dribbled down from the "white folks"—which is to say, the responsible ruling class—was that the white girls allegedly raped on a freight train near Scottsboro were "trash" and that the colored boys who allegedly did it were put up to it by communist outsiders trying to stir up trouble. These "Communists" were usually linked to the "N-Double-A-C-P," which was contemptuously dismissed as a "nigger front for communist Jews" and which had no known membership in Limestone County where I lived.

Oddly enough, it was only after I left Alabama in 1941 that I met any real Communists, but when I did, there turned out to be a prospective southern connection. On my first job in Chicago, at a large North Side hospital, I was almost immediately surrounded by new white "friends" who invited me to their parties and took me to rallies to "free Earl Browder" and to lectures by Elizabeth Gurley Flynn. They proposed a free college education for me in Russia if I would join the Young Communists' League and agree to return to Alabama and work for the party after my Russian education was completed. When I shared the news of this amazing opportunity with Jay Wright, my erstwhile Yankee principal (now expatriated from Alabama, as was I, but still in touch), his response was immediate if not altogether reassuring. The universities in Chicago, he said, were better than anything they had in Leningrad, and if I graduated from one of them, I would be under no obligation to go to Alabama or anywhere else to pay for my education. In the meantime, he thought he could obtain a scholarship for me at one of the black colleges in the South. He did, and I went. But even in college in the South, I never did encounter anybody who had any known connections with or any advocacy of communism.

Cash's reading of the black response to the issue of communism is essentially correct. First, it was an *ism*, an ideology. Black people have learned by bitter experience that ideology and its realization are two different things, and even if the ends of ideology are accomplished, they have a way of vanishing or withering away long before the black estate is benefited. The African American's cold response to communism was not so much a matter of insufficient resentment against things as they were as it was the instinctive realization that it was an ism designed by and for white people, whose primary concern, despite their protestations to the contrary, was their own peculiar interests. Their promise to erase the centuries-old color line and their eager demonstrations to prove their sincerity flew in the face of experience and ran counter to the instincts of survival. Moreover, critical to the black sense of survival was God, who in the black experience had proven himself more powerful than any ideology and more reliable than any ideologue. Cash calls the communist dream of black involvement "foolish" and "fatuous" in the supposition "that white men of the lower orders could be persuaded to join with [Blacks] against their ruling kin." How much more foolish and fatuous must have been the expectations that Blacks, whose whole history of past survival and whose expectations for future relief in America were anchored in their faith in God, his justice, and his grace, were going to switch loyalties on the specious lure of white social acceptance! Hence, if the mind of the South seriously entertained the fear of communist-based Negro equality, then the southern claim to "know the Negro" (a convention that never had much credibility) had completely disgraced itself. Black communism was never a threat to the South, or the North, or anywhere else in America. Like other possibilities in a situation so critical that no possibility could be ignored, it was embraced by a few, a very few, but it was never the great hope of the black masses. Nor could it ever be. God got there first.

THE MIND OF RELIGION

This brings us inevitably to the question of religion and derivative concepts in the official mind Cash writes about. His ruminations on this subject are disconcerting to say the least, and pursued to their logical conclusion they raise dire and troublesome questions about the locus of moral responsibility in the mind of the South.

According to Cash, the southern mentality is informed by two conflicting, compelling interests—puritanism and hedonism. But curiously, these "incompatible tendencies . . . [never] come into open and decisive contention" and are "without conscious imposture." More curious still is Cash's categorical denial of hypocrisy. "Far from it," he insists. Perhaps "a sort of social schizophrenia," he admits with measured reluctance, but "more simply and more safely . . . it was all part and parcel of that naïve capacity for unreality which was characteristic of him" (i.e., the southerner). If Cash is right, then the unfortunate southerner of whatever class is to be more pitied than blamed, for he is a mere creature of the characteristic unrealities through which he views the world, and no less the subject of his unrestrained passions than the savage African he charged himself, as the left hand of God, to tame and civilize. How abysmally tragic that is, if true; but Gunnar Myrdal, who wrote on the American mentality about the same time as Cash, was considerably less accepting. Myrdal found the incongruity between religious precept and moral performance so disturbing that he labeled it a national dilemma characteristic of American behavior, the South not excepted. If Myrdal is creditable, then Cash walks the narrow rim of casuistry. History is still assessing the effects (if not the culpability) of the South's prolonged commitment to an inordinate self-indulgence protected by some miraculous, immanent immunity lodged securely in its private imaginings. Above the noisome debate it has engendered, the burden of that commitment still falls where it always did—on the unfortunates who, if they were ever aware that it was taking place, were seldom permitted to address it.

In the long run, however, the ultimate impairment must lie in the redefinition of the religion that was once thought by many to be the common worldview undergirding the Republic, without reference to race or region (and by the grace of God), and to be clearly within the capabilities of all Americans of reasonable understanding. After so many centuries of sober acceptance it is disquieting to be suddenly challenged with the possibility that those Americans most avid and most demonstrable in their religious commitment were, alas, by some irreversible tragic flaw, barred from the realization of their spiritual efforts and blind to the realities of their own delinquency.

Could this be the burden of Cash's apologetic? I do not think so. The disarming candor with which he approaches even the most intimate foibles of the southern mind suggest an earnestness and sincerity that must not be discredited on this troublesome issue of moral schizophrenia, critical as it is to the understanding of a pattern of behavior with such awesome consequences for so many millions of people for so many hundreds of years. Yet, if Cash's assessment of the southerner's moral naïveté is taken at face value, then this whole appraisal of the mind of the South seems a gratuitous exercise. It cannot mean anything, because the people he writes about are rendered puppets of forces over which they have no control, involved in the pursuit of a spectrum of manifest behavior that can have no moral consequences. Hence the roasting of a nigger and the roasting of a shoat are alike experiences in the same spectrum of plausibility. And blaming the Yankee for making the South hate Negroes is acceptable logic in a worldview of such distressed realities. The strange psychological gymnastics (so troublesome to contemporary apologists) that "explain" how a Christian "master" could beget children by the black women he owned and controlled, declare them surplus, and sell them for money suddenly clicks into focus when seen through W. J. Cash's prism of the mind of the South. And the taboo that forbids to this day any recognition of kinship between the millions of blacks and whites who continue to share the southern region a hundred years or more after the last African American innocent of "Colonel Bascombe's" meanderings was born there, underscores the intensity with which the mind of the South remains successfully battened down against the obvious, and remains contemptuous of any logic not its own. But sooner or later logic has a way of managing its own manifestation. There is an Ashanti proverb that reminds us: "If you sow wild peppers to the wind, they will sprout around your feet."

THE RULING MIND

Despite his courage in trying to offer a plausible analysis of his own cultural roots, W. J. Cash was fettered by the very conventions and perceptions he labored to explain. He was a creature of his own times and his own class, and he was sacked in the same spiritual hairshirt that afflicted the people he wrote about. In consequence, his commitment to the illusion that the ruling mind is the only mind of moment is instinctive, but the lessons of history—ancient, recent, and contemporary—must not be permitted to stand for nothing.

> Nations and empires rise and decline
> Princes and prelates rule for a day.[3]

The ruling mind is not invulnerable to the vagaries of change; and even when change appears to be precipitous and without reasonable cause, in the province of human affairs the evidences of previously unrecognized cerebral ferment will likely surface in the afterbirth. There is no smoke until the gun is fired.

At the very time Cash was being hailed for his disclosure of the traditional establishment mind of the South, a countermind that was destined to change the South forever was taking on definition

3. "Return O Lord," in C. Eric Lincoln, *This Road since Freedom* (Durham: Carolina Wren, 1990), p. 59.

in the form of the civil rights revolution. It was a different mind-set that ere long would augur a somber reappraisal of that "ancient and docile" Negro the white South contended it knew so well. A new and unanticipated reality was looming on the horizon, and the Negro the ruling mind knew so well got up from his knees in graceless betrayal of that dogma. Suddenly a mind admitted to exist only in the embryonic craftiness of an Uncle Remus was about to break through the carefully crafted iron mesh of three centuries of political and cultural restraint in a public demonstration of maturity and independence, and the stubborn rigidity with which the ruling mind of the South dismissed lesser minds would be painfully ruptured. The cultivated obliviousness of the Nat Turners, David Walkers, Frederick Douglasses, Harriet Tubmans, Richard Allens, and Henry M. Turners in favor of a more comforting vision of darkies in the cotton singing away their miseries proved shortsighted in the long run, and it left the South ill-prepared to confront, and worse prepared to understand, the sudden arrival of the future on the heels of World War II.

The truth is that the future symbolized by *Brown v. Board of Education,* which seemed to fall on Dixie like an intruding comet in 1954, trailing fire and ice all across America, was not a cataclysmic arrival at all. There had always been *that other mind.* There had always been that muted countermind, denied expression, but there nonetheless. There is such a mind in every repressed society, building its venires, weighing its options, waiting to be heard. Such is the lesson implicit in the disintegration of the Soviet empire and the transfer of political power in South Africa, where the ruling mind ran to the rigidity of place called apartheid while the countermind was bent on freedom. The time must come for the people to be heard, "or the very stones will cry out." It has been fifty years, a scant half century, since Cash's southern exposure titillated the literati, baffled the historians, and gratified the folks back home. He probably convinced no one, least of all those missing from his assessment of what really mattered and who made that determination. America has changed a lot since then. The industries that brought progress to the South are now taking that progress to Mexico and Korea. The cotton mills that damned the unions, exploited the poor whites, and disdained the Negroes have gone to Hong Kong and Taiwan. The communism the South fretted about is in serious decline all over the world and has long been a dead horse and a dead issue in the catalog of black political aspiration. The Ku Klux Klan, that alleged "authentic folk movement," is authentic no longer. It never was, but it remains nonetheless a public shrine for the rallying of a diverse collectivity of unrepentant chauvinists unwilling to accept any part of the painfully wrought, still emergent new dispensation history has decreed for any world we may know tomorrow. This new dispensation is symbolized in America by the transition of those same muted black voices singing in the cotton yesterday, who are found increasingly in more respected environments today, sharing with their erstwhile "keepers" the delicate decisions determining the welfare of a common constituency.

Better education at all levels and a less restrictive mobility render the old conventional social typologies and classifications increasingly hazardous and unreliable, although a still formidably resistant color line remains the covert arbiter of race and place. But today if you rub the carefully "home folks" patina of the southern professional or businessman, as likely as not you will find a transplanted Yankee. The mind of the South that Cash wrote about, the mind that imagined itself to be the projection of the Virginia aristocracy, or of origins equally distinctive, would be hard put to explain what is happening in Virginia and elsewhere in the South today because the old distinctions between the "best people," "the common people," and the "trash" are increasingly blurred. What is more, the "good ol' boys" who used to be dismissed as trash have modified their image and their style. Once they draw the curtains of the voting booth, they are as likely to vote Republican as they are to hew to the line that once made the South "solid" in politics and sentiment alike.

The Solid South has gone the way of the bustle. It exists only in the memory of the most nostalgic romantics. Among the remaining critical symbols of Cash's mind of the South, the cult of white womanhood, though still among the most sacred gargoyles guarding the heroic fantasies of the southern white male, has been grievously threatened and confused—not by the lust of the savage African but by the determination of the southern white woman herself. She has dared to trade in her romantic pedestal for the level ground of the office, the courtroom, the pulpit, the marketplace, the halls of academe, and wherever else the appreciation of her mind (rather than her symbol) will take her. It was her decision to make, and she made it. If there is any attendant trauma, it does not appear to be hers.

THE BLACK CHURCH

Finally, in the fifty-odd years since Cash published *The Mind of the South,* the decline of religion and of the church as the principal arbiter of social behavior and social acceptability is perhaps the most critical index of a region in the throes of change. That the whole nation has taken a serious turn toward secularity is one thing, but the notion that the South could ever be a part of that same spiritual erosion is another. The South has always counted itself God's special sanctuary, and upon that notion rested the principal foundation stones of that region's call to travail and suffering, its oblique reading of righteousness and providential trust, and its expectation of a triumphant Armageddon in the end. Under the leadership of a class of pontifical preachers who obligingly capped the free will and individual responsibility of Methodism with the fixed destiny of Calvinism, the hedonism the South could not abandon and the puritanism it could not escape were forced to live together in the same house, but the South could find in that arrangement a divine sanction for an otherwise improbable reading of Christian responsibility and spiritual health. So emerged a tribal deity safely unsusceptible to the childish complaints of the heathen Africans or to the nervous yowlings of the Yankees and all others not bona fide supplicants at the shrine of southern destiny.

It was the fixity of divine decree that established the proper place for everyone who was a participant in God's scheme of things. Critical to this arrangement and its maintenance was the preacher, the vicegerent of the tribal deity charged with the ordering of the society through the ordering of the faith in accordance with the order of the preferences and responsibilities mutually understood and agreed upon. It was the preacher who could stave off God's wrath or bring on God's blessings. It was the preacher who could invoke an eternity of hellfire and damnation upon the spiritual sluggards—the evil-minded Yankees, the black sons of Ham, and all others who implicitly or explicitly challenged the Way of the Chosen as interpreted by those called to that task.

But change did not favor the side of the cloth. Ecumenism in the form of denominational mergers transcending the demographics of politics and personal preferences weakened the absolutism of the local preachers and forced the recognition (if not the consideration) of ideas and ideologies that were sometimes alien to the southern temper. Southern and northern Baptists, Methodists, and Presbyterians who had gone their separate ways a hundred years earlier over the "unreconcilable" issues of the Civil War did find reconciliation after all (mutatis mutandis, of course). And even the Blacks who were the root cause of the century-old schisms found new arrangements of sorts for their accommodation in the reconstituted churches, should they choose to accept them. The vast majority did not, of course, opting overwhelmingly in favor of the black denominations, which found little recognition and less consideration in the official mind of the South. But the black church had a mind of its own. It was the genesis, the womb, the sustainer, and the projector of the countermind that would eventually challenge the ruling mind of the South, and would ultimately humanize its determinations in the interest of a new southern temper that W. J. Cash would surely find revelational if he were to undertake a new assessment of the mind of the South today.

IV

POLYPS
OF
PREJUDICE

America

In God We Trust

If God is worthy, God is Just

Did God fail in His creative task

Does black some Godly error mask?

—C. ERIC LINCOLN,

This Road since Freedom

America has a problem with Alexander Hamilton, the first secretary of the United States Treasury. The problem has nothing to do with whether Alexander Hamilton performed adequately in the role which history assigned to him. That he was a "Founding Father" of consequence considerably beyond mere adequacy seems well established. He also headed a corporation, founded a town, and fought one of the most celebrated pistol duels in American history. *But was he black?* That is less well established, and his relevance and his *proper* place in history remain undetermined until we know for sure. On that pretext some Americans would have him disinterred. Although Mr. Hamilton has long since gone to his spiritual reward, there remains for us, the living, the troublesome issue of whether the halo of his greatness might somehow lose its glow if his genes were tainted and his color uncertified. How terrible it would be to find out after two hundred years that he was racially incapable of being who he was or doing what he did!

The Alexander Hamilton syndrome is a trenchant reminder that the American people are as sensitive to race today as they ever were, and that the alleged declining significance of race in the distribution of good, goods, and the good life in America is illusory. We have indeed developed amazingly adroit sophistications of language and style, but we still want to know before we are prepared to make any significant commitment: *Is he white or, is she black?*

It is a commonplace assumption that blacks are "different" from ordinary people. They are not *extraordinary*, of course, just different. So if they excel in baseball or track or basketball or football, it is because they are *anatomically* different. They've got longer legs, or bigger thighs, or five-chambered hearts, or other primordial equipment necessary to predatory survival, so if they can run faster or jump higher than others it is because their primitive origins have not yet been transcended by Wester-style civilization. Hence their intellectual development is no more than is enough to service their physical needs and interests. Because a benevolent Mother Nature has matched intellectual capacity with Blacks' self-perceived needs, there are limits to what they can accomplish in a more advanced civilization, and it is futile to expect them to accomplish what they are obviously not equipped to do. In keeping with this conventional article of faith, each generation produces a new spate of Jencks-and-Reisman scholars, by whatever name, who, armed with a formidable arsenal of charts and statistics, climb out of the ivy to reassure us that the status is still quo as far as African American development is concerned. The gap between black performance and white achievement is still an ordinance of nature, we learn anew, and African American underperformance has nothing whatever to do with the structure or requirements of the social order.

Come now Richard Herrnstein and Charles Murray with the latest "bell curve" for the Jencksian tradition, but what it seems to measure most accurately is the pervasive yearning for a scientific justification of an entrenched social practice that is neither scientific nor just.

How high does your IQ have to be to steal a million dollars from charity? To kill 168 people in a public building? To feed placebos to dying patients who think they are being treated? And if ever we find to our complete satisfaction that all African Americans do in fact have lower IQs than all white Americans, just what will we do about it? Will we bar them from public office (or public housing)? Will we refuse to issue them marriage licenses or require legal termination of all blighted cases in utero? Or will we require "voluntary" sterilization? Will we set aside special spaces or places for our intellectually disabled citizens so that the "able" will always have reserved emergency parking available? I am not aware that a satisfactory IQ, which is itself still a debatable, subjective construct, is as yet a determinant of significance in what it means to be human. The IQ is a post hoc evaluation which can only be made *after* the fact of humanity with all of its inalienable rights and expectations has been confirmed by other, less susceptible measurements. So unless we harbor some dark Hitlerian ambitions about the development of a super race, one wonders what the ever-recurrent fuss is really all about. The human species is rife with spectrums of difference, nature's distribution of attributes, as must be evident to even the most casual observer. The issue is not whether we differ: obviously we do. The issue is whether that difference makes any difference in the human obligation to recognize itself in the proper recognition of every human being.

If we take a random sample of names recently in the news, like Jonas Salk, who invented penicillin; Martin Luther King, Jr., civil rights leader; Jeffrey Dahmer, the serial killer who stored and ate some of his quarry; Colin Powell, former chair of the Joint Chiefs of Staff; Marcia Clark, Los Angeles deputy district attorney; Timothy McVeigh, accused of mass murder in the 1995 Oklahoma City bombing; Marian Wright Edelman, children's rights advocate; and Malcolm X, Muslim religious guru, we have a reasonable cross section of white and black achievement in America. I have no idea how they would rank on an IQ chart, but according to the public press they seem to have accomplished with efficiency and dispatch whatever they determined to have significance or value. Is this intelligence? Is this *the sum* of intelligence, or is there something more? Or possibly something less? Whatever it is that the intelligence quotient claims to measure or predict, sooner or later its true believers must grapple with the question of sufficiency; that is, *What is the minimum IQ required to retain the right to be a person in this society?* And how shall we deal with those who fail (by our standards) to make the cut? The presumptive candidates have already been chosen, it seems, and they are not among the test makers. Nevertheless, it is interesting to note that the "Eve hypothesis" of contemporary genetics theory holds that we are all descended from a small population of African women. Yet another theory, advanced by geneticist Robert Dorritt, claims, based on the evidence of one genetic marker on the Y chromosome, that we are all descended from a small group of African men. Adam or Eve, take your pick, if modern science is to be trusted we may all be African by derivation.

That issue of such critical moment reminds me of how my grandmother dealt with similar issues of consequence. On Sundays when times were good we frequently had a visiting preacher for dinner after church. Grandma was as famous for her cooking as she was for her candor, and her Sunday dinner was carefully cooked and set aside before we went to eleven o'clock service. All but the cornbread, her specialty. That was always served hot from the oven. If the clergyman coming to dinner was in her estimation a first-rate preacher, she always put *two* eggs into the cornbread she made for him, denoting her favorable estimate of the way he handled his spiritual craft. If she rated him mediocre or only average, she served him *one*-egg bread. She always treated one-egg and two-egg preachers with the same Christian deference, but it was important to her to make her personal evaluations on professional merit, and to signify her appraisal through a private culinary protocol that demeaned no one. Contemporary Americans don't like to guess who's coming to dinner either, but we operate on the assumption that if you don't hear the preaching, you won't need to crack *any* eggs and you can have your dinner all to yourself.

It is this preemptive rush to judgment on race that makes Alexander Hamilton symbolically important beyond his accomplishments as a statesman. Though he has long since been laid to rest, the culture remains restive over the unresolved question of *what color* he was rather than *what* he was, or the quality of his contribution to his country. It is neither my task nor my competence to add to this tempest in a snuffbox. Rather, my concern is how we live with the paradox of racism in a world and a society in which it is generally admitted that people are somehow people, and all share together a common species and a common origin and a common fate. In such a society, the Alexander Hamilton syndrome would seem illogical and irrational on its face. But then, one of the earliest things we learn about human beings is that their designation as *Homo sapiens*—"intelligent beings"— notwithstanding, they can be exasperatingly illogical and doggedly irrational; and that race, or the imagination of it, has but one close rival in the production of human destructiveness and misery. There is no issue, save possibly religion, which in the light of historical experience has proven so capable of envenomizing humanity. And when religion and race are paired in determining *who does not belong,* as has been the case so many times in the long history of what we are pleased to call human development, the results have been disastrous, and the retardation of human progress has been costly beyond imagination. World War II is a case in point. The self-styled Aryans focused upon the Jews, who had a distinctive religion to add to their already Aryan-perceived racial deficits. The ensuing holocaust was unparalleled in the whole history of humankind for its ferocity, its barbarity, its gruesomeness, and its spite. Humanity was suspended and civilization took a holiday while a people noted for its genius in art, music, religion, philosophy, science, and letters reverted to savagery and all but destroyed a people equally accomplished. It was all a matter of race, or the conviction that race is real and a value worth killing for.

THE NOTION OF RACE

What is this thing called race, this pervasive concept which sets humans against each other with such consummate virulence and passion? Race means different things to different people, of course, and we could easily exhaust both patience and possibility without making a serious dent in the panoply of racial ideology, or without coming to any substantial agreement about what lies behind it. Let it suffice to say that race is essentially a biological concept, which implies that the *physical* characteristics which members of the group have in common are genetically determined. In consequence, a biologist or anthropologist who talks about race is talking about hair texture, skin color, the shape of the head, blood type, and so on; but not about intelligence or mental ability, because these have not been racially determined. The scientific concept of race completely excludes from consideration any characteristics that are entirely the result of external environmental influences and not the consequences of heredity.[1] Skin color is a phenomenon which varies across a wide spectrum among human types, as any casual observer will admit. Contemporary breakthroughs in genetics refer to race as "a population which differs significantly from some other human populations in regard to the frequency of one or more of the genes it possesses."[2] This means that science has abandoned the old three-tiered groupings of Mongoloid, Caucasoid, and Negroid for a much more sophisticated taxonomy. By the early 1960s as many as thirty-four races had been identified. By now, thanks to our increasingly refined understanding of what it means to be human, the old fantasies about racial distinctions are hopelessly obsolete. We are only what we are, and race can never be more than a subgrouping of a single species with a genetically open system. Our genes have been interchanged for thousands of years, and there is no reason to believe that such intermixing will be discontinued any time soon. There is no genetic barrier to racial intermixing, and no physiological or mental penalty imposed by nature. This fact alone makes the notion of race as a discrete, distinguishable human population a myth and a fantasy. When an Alabama high school principal canceled the 1994 Senior Prom at his school to avoid interracial dating, a student of mixed parentage who questioned his logic was told that *she* "was a mistake"! To take seriously the implications of that evaluation is to conclude that the United States, which began as "a nation of immigrants," has now become "a nation of errors." Type O blood from a Zulu in South Africa could well save the life of the most arrogant Aryan in Berlin having blood of the same type, while a different type of blood drawn from a fellow "Aryan" might very well kill him. That *would* be a mistake. And irreversible.

COLOR

It has been said that anybody who attempts to make a critical judgment about an individual strictly on the basis of color

1. Anthony H. Richmond, *The Colour Problem* (Baltimore: Penguin Books, rev., 1961), p. 13.
2. Martin Deutsch et al., eds., *Social Class, Race, and Psychological Development* (New York: Holt, Rinehart and Winston, 1968), pp. 12, 13.

is either mad or a fool, because color varies intensely within every subgroup and is probably the least reliable index of any schedule of values, including racial identity itself. Nevertheless, in spite of its many contraindications—religious, moral, legal, and humanitarian—color became a cardinal fixation quite early in the American cultural development, and it has been retained as a principal basis for the arbitrary assignment of scarce values ever since. Color is the critical determiner of who may and who may not belong, who may and who may not serve, who may and who may not be served, and who may or may not be considered respectable.

HOW DID WE GET THIS WAY?

There are those who profess to believe that there is a natural antipathy built into the human psyche which impels racial groups to shun each other and to keep to themselves. If that is true, children apparently don't know about it, because they play together without inhibition up to the age of adult contamination. Young adults don't seem to have it either, because in spite of the most fervent indoctrination, proscription, and the harshest of social penalties, they seem to manage the inevitable liaisons which make a mockery of so-called racial purity all over the world. If, indeed, nature has provided us with such a psychological prophylaxis, one wonders why so many laws and conventions are aimed at preventing what nature has already denied. I, for one, am willing to concede Mother Nature's priority and experience in the business of human construction and control. And I am impressed with her proven proficiency in taking care of the "unnatural" in all other instances with intricate barriers or troublesome penalties which make the proscribed activity extremely hazardous, burdensome, or impossible. So we must look further than "nature" for support of our wistful commitment to a two-tiered humanity. If such was ever a part of Mother Nature's scheme for humanity, she abandoned it too long ago for us to dream of its recovery.

DEROGATION AND CONFIRMATION

Primary identity is nonnegotiable; it is genealogically determined. But functional identity is in part conditioned by the perceptions of significant others, and in this society, color, the least reliable index to one's value as a human being, is burdened with an impossible task of evaluation and prediction, not only for individuals but for the whole culture.

When Benjamin Disraeli's political enemies wanted to discredit him, they placed a picture of an African beside a likeness of Disraeli and invited the public to draw their own conclusions. And in the United States, just before the 1920 presidential elections, the political opponents of Warren G. Harding leaked it to the press that Mr. Harding was a Negro. During World War II, Hitler's New York-born propagandist, Lord Haw Haw, charged that Winston Churchill's mother was an "American Negress," and that his father, Lord Randolph Churchill, died of an unmentionable disease, thus doubly damning the prime minister and his fitness to lead the British people. Hitler himself dismissed American civilization as inferior because it had been "mongrelized" by centuries of race mixing. But Herr Hitler, like most demagogues, was exceedingly selective in his reading of history. Armies footnote their passage with progeny, and the continent of Europe has had more than its share of marauding conquerors. Long before America came into existence the invasions of the Mongols, the Muslims, the Moors, and other military adventurers deflowered the myths of racial purity on the continent of Europe. Indeed, the Roman armies with their legions of swarthy soldiers from Africa and Asia distributed some very uncharacteristic gene pools as far north as England and Scandinavia quite early in the development of European civilization, and the African impact on the Iberian Peninsula and southern Europe lingers to this day in the visage of the Spaniard, the Sicilian, the Portuguese, and other nationalities clustered around the Mediterranean Basin.

Genes know nothing of policies or politics, but the truth is sometimes made manifest in curious ways and unexpected places, as if to remind us that nature has a larger agenda transcending the pettiness and the inconsistencies of pride and prejudice which dog the human cavalcade. So Greece was blessed (or damned, as the case may be) with Aesop, the fabulist; Germany with Beethoven, the composer; France with Alexandre Dumas, the novelist;

Russia with Pushkin, the poet; Maryland with Benjamin Banneker, the inventor and astronomer; Connecticut with Lemuel Haynes, distinguished clergyman and missionary; and Washington, D.C., with Patrick Francis Healy, the Jesuit priest who was president of Georgetown University from 1873 to 1882.

What did Beethoven and Dumas, Pushkin and Banneker, Haynes and Father Healy have in common? They were all of African descent, they were all touched with genius, and they were all significant contributors to cultures in which they were visible minorities. There is an even deeper lesson implicit in all this: If genius marks only a few, and fewer still come to public attention, what we see may be only the tip of the iceberg that represents a massive potential which we do not permit ourselves to see or even to contemplate.

In 1958 scientists at Ohio State University estimated that at least twenty-eight million *white* Americans were partially of African descent.[3] Almost four decades have passed since then, and it is a reasonable speculation that even when allowance is made for the relatively low rate of reproduction among American whites, and most particularly in the light of drastically relaxed sexual mores, the number of white Americans endowed with substantial numbers of genes of African derivation must be near, or perhaps already exceeds, one hundred million. The other shoe was dropped by Professor I. I. Gottesman, a biogeneticist at the University of Minnesota, who reasons that "from a biological point of view, it is nonsensical to label someone with the remotest trace of Negro ancestry as a member of the Negro race. African American gene pools contain from 10 to 25 percent white genes." This corresponds, Professor Gottesman continues, "to having a white grandfather or great-grandfather. If you choose to call the white individual with a Negro grandfather a Negro, then logic would require you to call the 'average' Negro in New York or Baltimore white."[4]

3. Deutsch et al., *Social Class, Race, and Psychological Development*, p. 12.
4. Ibid., pp. 21–22.

But alas! Racism is anything but logical, and sex is more likely than reason to be color-blind. Long before our belated attempts at "desegregation," it would have been practically impossible to fill a lunch counter anywhere in America with black people of "pure" African descent. And as the generations succeed each other, the old racial shibboleths about who is coming to dinner or who is running for president can hardly be serviced by the most efficient technology we are likely to have available. From Thomas Jefferson, who took his black consort, Sally Hemings, all the way to Paris to ease the loneliness of his ambassadorship, to Jefferson Davis and his alleged incestuous liaison with his brother Joe's daughter by a slave woman, to the lost statistics of the contemporary college dating game, the racial restructuring of America has been and is under constant modification while our formal attitudes about race and place always seem to remain constant. In 1900 the Manassa Society of Chicago, an organization for members of interracial marriages, had more than seven hundred members. The Census Bureau listed 164,000 black-white families in 1983, and the number of such unions is certainly increasing, as is the number of fair-complexioned Blacks who "pass" by simply dropping out of one race and moving into the other, compounding the problem of racial bookkeeping for those who make their critical decisions on the basis of such data. The squeamish should not look too hard or scratch too deeply. What you see is what you get. What you got may not be what you were looking for, but then, that's the way America is, and aren't we all Americans?

THE URGE TO MERGE
At a time before American idealism learned to discipline itself, the expectation was that this new outpost of Western development was destined to become a supercivilization of European cultural eclecticism under the preemptive imprimatur of the Anglo-Saxon experience. The rhetoric of politics and the premature conclusions of untested social theory proclaimed America to be a vast melting pot from which countless millions of immigrant Poles, Czechs, Hungarians, Irish, Italians, Jews, and the like would emerge as a new and singular people after proper annealing in

the cauldron of Americanization. There would be but one aim, one name: *American!* Was it not Emma Lazarus, a Spanish Jew, who wrote the official welcome a self-confident America caused to be inscribed on the Statue of Liberty, the national symbol of our belief in our destiny to mold and give to the world a new people?

> Give me your tired your poor
> your huddled masses
> yearning to breathe free.

Yes. And so they came, by the millions—among them Jews in search of the ancient promise of being uniquely themselves even in America. But for most of the others who came, all that was required was the urge to merge—to "melt," as it were, and be one with the developing American archetype.

As things turned out, however, there were some for whom the urge to merge held no attraction. They left the Old Country less with the intent of being molded into the New American than with the hope of having increased opportunities for remaining who they were. The process of being shorn of treasured cultural or ethnic identity and melted into a homogenized general population turned out to be more stressful and less rewarding than some "new Americans" had bargained for, and they paid the price for their recalcitrance.

Others found the melting process to exist mainly in the imaginations of its true believers. There were barriers to assimilation, and some of them were formidable. Perhaps it could be so for their children, or for their children's children, but not for themselves. For them, maybe it would be better to give priority to immediate, visceral needs—keeping to their own communities, looking after their own. These immigrants, too, paid a price—for their caution.

For the true believers, assimilation was the narrow gate to the real America and to being real Americans. It was the surest access to the American Dream. If the annealing process was slow and uncertain, it could be catalyzed by certain strategies guaranteed to close the gap between the dream and reality. For example, if one were both enterprising and committed, one could swallow a troublesome accent, convert to a new religion, and learn to get along without the last syllable of the family name. If the dream was worth more than identity, one could adopt a new name altogether. And to make the conversion complete, one could forswear the comforts of endogamy and take a spouse from the reference group of which one intended to be a part.

The point is that *some* could be melted and assimilated, but like so many other theories about how people *ought* to behave, the melting pot theory of American assimilation was notable for its exceptions. It was not an adequate projection of what could (and did) happen to millions of European immigrants, and it did not address itself at all in any serious way to the black experience in America. For African Americans, the urge to merge was a cynical Cinderella ball which they were expected to prepare and service, but to which they were never to be invited. It was the *great lie* that is still dredged up to explain to a willfully credulous America why some have made it here, and some have not.

At the height of the European exodus to America, in the late nineteenth century, African Americans already constituted a sizable indigenous population. But they were not, by reason of certain continuing disabilities, real or imagined, assimilated into the general population. Merely to call them "American" was to observe a political courtesy scarcely grounded in the security of true citizenship. It did not seem to matter that they already spoke the established language, having learned it over three centuries or so of intimate proximity and experience, when so many of their European counterparts required two or three generations to use English with facility. The African Americans had no telltale accents, only the approved regional inflections of the indigenous old stock. Since they were already Methodists and Baptists by faith, there was little need for Blacks to apostatize; (although convention has it that Episcopalianism was, in the case of the more assiduous European immigrants, the religion of choice for people being melted at the bottom with hopes of being assimilated at the top).

And black people did not need to worry about changing their

names. They had good, euphonious "American" names already, without any troublesome suffixes like *witz* or *berg* or *stein* or *sky*. Their names had been gratuitously lent to them in recognition of the property interest they once implied. As for exogamy as a strategy of assimilation, in most states Blacks were prevented by law (and relentlessly discouraged by convention) from any marriage options except endogamy. Nevertheless, wherever law or custom contrives to exclude arbitrarily selected populations from the common generic indulgence, an alternative circuitry to achieve the denied values will almost certainly be developed. And so it was with the African Americans from the earliest days of slavery. Human ingenuity will find a way in, or at least a way not to be totally shut out. However annoying to the gatekeepers, or hazardous to the gate creepers, the need to be "inside" will assert itself. So it was that while others changed their names and their religions, assimilation-minded Blacks simply changed their "race." They "passed," and they still do.

BLACKS AND JEWS

Our present concern is limited to that vast majority of Blacks and Jews who, for whatever reason, remained Blacks and Jews. They are the principals in the play within the play. Once our two most prominent minorities, they are still the ones most often engaged in a bittersweet encounter which makes the front page of the daily press and the prime-time news on the television set, thus giving a distinctive profile to the nature of prejudice in America. But the pursuit of the American Dream has been on different terms and under highly disparate restraints and conditions, and Blacks and Jews have arrived at their present locations via different routes and through a vastly different set of protocols. Historically, African Americans have simply wanted to be *Americans,* but American racism has always negated that possibility, or made it conditional. In consequence, it may be time to rethink the whole question of black identity and its meaning in America. Historically, Jews too have wanted to be Americans, but they have always insisted as well on retaining their Jewishness. From the point of view of most Jews, the options for entering the American mainstream at the sacrifice of religious and cultural identity were scarcely viable. There is recent evidence, however, that the traditional priority on Jewish identity has declined significantly among some contemporary Jewish youth. But to black people the feeling that the Jew can have it both ways is a part of the reality that shapes the Black-Jew encounter. They can be "white" when they choose to be, and they can be "Jewish" when being white is inconvenient. But the Jew is *never* black. Hence, to black people whatever disabilities the Jew suffers seem voluntary and relative.

While such a view is undoubtedly simplistic, it is true that anti-Semitism in America has always been comparatively mild in comparison with the massive denial of black aspiration for full community. In the first place, the American dislike for the Jew was a secondary reaction. Jewish oppression was something that occurred elsewhere—in the ghettos of Europe. Americans learned about it secondhand. There were no historical patterns or origins for anti-Semitism in America except by vicarious association. On the other hand, racism, for all practical purposes, *originated* in America. It produced an institution by means of which white people enslaved black people and have sought continuously since to justify that behavior. As a consequence of this primary, personal experience, guilt, fear, and the need for vindication all contributed to the severity of the oppression directed toward African Americans. To the degree that Jews have remembered their own historic bondage and oppression and their behavior toward Blacks is informed by that recollection, they have reason to expect that behavior to be recognized and respected in turn.

Blacks and Jews are no strangers to each other. Their cultural interface transcends continents and centuries alike, and reaches deep into the mantle of antiquity which gave to each a distinctive identity and a separate development in a transcendent scenario which is still unfolding. Jews are Jews, and Blacks are Blacks, but one inscrutable finger that moves and writes of its own volition and purpose keeps the record books for both. In the compelling search for their respective destinies, Blacks and Jews have found themselves dispersed throughout the world as involuntary instruments in the self-perceived destinies of others. The history of their travail is the somber documentation of the tenuousness of the human commitment to its own ideals whenever that commitment scuffs against the idolatry of race and ethnicity. What they have learned should make them wary; what they have experienced should make them charitable; and what they know should make them leaders in the difficult transformation America must make from an outdated monoculture to a society that must be equitably inclusive in the days ahead. Destiny is still in process. History is not yet done.

The black man's visibility made him a ready, constant target, and if the popular view that the Jew can change identities like a chameleon is overdrawn, it at least has a basis in fact. White is the color of privilege in America. *Anybody* who is white is automatically *presumed* to warrant certain prerogatives, privileges, and preferences over anybody who is black. Jews do not have to take advantage of their color. They are born with it, and American convention has made of it a value of enormous potential. In consequence, some Jews will go to great pains to make it clear that Jews are *white,* and that being white they will, as individuals, behave more or less like other whites.

It is interesting, however, that traditionally, African Americans have made their own distinction between "Jews" and "whites." For better or for worse, most Blacks think of Jews in terms of what is perceived as their cultural and religious projections, and black conventions almost never indiscriminately lump Jews with Caucasians. The conventional reference in black folklore is to whites *and* Jews. In most instances this has permitted an interpretation of racial attitudes and behaviors toward Blacks in which the Jew consistently appears less vicious and less brutal, if more cunning and deceitful. In recent times some new factors have emerged which tend to modify the black folklore perception and intensify the abrasiveness of the Black-Jew encounter. First of all, the Jews themselves have increasingly stressed their "white" identity, and they have become increasingly visible in the white power structure. At the same time Jewish allegations of black anti-Semitism seem to hinge increasingly on disparate political postures regarding the state of Israel. At the more personal level, the competition between Blacks and Jews has increased sharply since the civil rights revolution opened new doors of possibility for both groups in public service, academe, and other places where Jews were usually restricted to quotas and Blacks were excluded altogether. Finally, the enormous growth in black Islam in the last thirty years is a phenomenon certain to feature prominently in new concepts of black identity and new political alliances and loyalties.

The new levels of acceptability enjoyed by contemporary Jews derive to a significant degree from the determined *black* civil rights crusade begun in the 1950s. Jewish money, Jewish legal expertise, and Jewish rank-and-file participation were important factors in the success of that movement, but if the Jews had done nothing at all, as a "white" minority they would still have reaped major benefits of the struggle before Blacks themselves could recognize any substantive change, because in America, upward mobility presupposes an order of priority in which African Americans are the presumptive candidates of last choice. Since Black Americans are the predetermined bottom of the heap, every other group has to be moved up and out if the pecking order is to be kept intact. While the hard boil of the Civil Rights movement was fired and fueled principally by Blacks, all the other disadvantaged minority sediments were stirred into the flux in the process. Those closest to the white Anglo-Saxon ideal (white women, for example) were the first ones precipitated to the crest of the boil and on out of the fire, as it were. Those considered farthest from that mythical ideal—African Americans in general and the black male in particular—are ostensibly still in the white heat of a white fire, and they will be among the last to reap the full benefits of the "liberation" they made possible for others.

For the Jew, the American Dream has taken on substantial form and substance. Overt acts of bigotry toward Jews have greatly diminished, the bars across the doors to Jewish success have for the most part been removed, and life is sweeter in America than anywhere else in the world. The American Dream is beginning to look like the stuff of reality. But for most African Americans, the dream is still a tantalizing will-o'-the-wisp chased over a hostile, impossible terrain. African Americans seem to be always chasing a dream that other Americans—who came so much later and paid so much less—always manage to realize much sooner than they do. Or as one despairing cynic put it, "If you're black, don't make no difference how long you work and how hard you sweat, when you reach for your pay there's gonna be somebody else' hand under yours."

For the overwhelming majority of African Americans, Jews qua Jews are not the adversary. They are only a familiar example of the viciousness of the pecking order in which Black Americans are the designated "It" for a game in which there are many underdogs but only one at the bottom, with no substantive repositioning in view.

The Black-Jew encounter is the record of two minorities trying to gain parity in a society which is intolerant of racial and cultural differences. Blacks and Jews are not the only groups involved in the struggle, although for the moment they continue to receive more media attention, but that will doubtless change as newer minorities move into the competition to be "next out of the fire." Blacks and Jews have pursued the American Dream with differing degrees of success, a matter determined by factors not within their control. Their separate struggles were defined by their separate identities, and rewarded or negated by the larger society from which they have both been excluded.

Just as Jews have never been considered by Blacks to be a focus of antiblack feeling, it is also true that classical anti-Semitism has never been a feature of black hostility. As a matter of fact, African Americans have, for most of their history, been so desperate in their efforts to establish their own humanity and their right to belong that there has been little energy left for hating *anybody*. The discrimination against African Americans has been so common, so harsh, and so unremitting that, incredible as it may seem, ordinary black people often did not know they were being discriminated against and could not identify the bigots if they did. A black woman who had lived all her life in Selma, Alabama, admitted that she had no sense of discrimination or oppression until Martin Luther King, Jr., went there. Differential treatment was so "normal" as to be unrecognized. Who, then, could single out Jews as a special target if they were behaving the way "white" people normally behave? If the Hungarians or the Poles took their jobs, or the Irish cop busted their skulls, or the "po' whites" lynched them while the "good whites" took their land, if the Jews exploited them financially and the Italians sold them bad meat and rotten produce, who were they going to single out to hate? *They hated themselves* for being the object of so much hatred.

Undoubtedly there is a greater sensitivity to the repositioning of interests throughout the society as the political face of America changes under the escalating impact of multiculturalism. This new determination to be involved in the whole spectrum of responsible citizenship is reflected in the growing black interest in international politics and an increasing insistence on the part of black leaders to see their constituencies in the context of world affairs. It is inevitable that new abrasions between Blacks and Jews (and Blacks and others) will develop as new liaisons are explored and fresh strategies for an old struggle are devised. The Old Order is changing—and will change—and conventional America may find the new resistance to convention to be, in a word, unconventional. The American profile must change with the changing times.

For those ransomed from the fire, Tacitus, that sage of the ancients, has left this reminder:

> Thus far you have known only adversity
> Prosperity tests the spirit with sharper goads
> For we endure misfortune
> But we are corrupted by success.

MINISTER LOUIS FARRAKHAN

A prominent irritant in the taut relations between African Americans and Jewish leaders is occasioned by the political rhetoric of Minister Louis Farrakhan. Mr. Farrakhan heads the Nation of Islam, an indigenous community of African American Muslims which came to prominence under the leadership of the late Honorable Elijah Muhammed and Malcolm X. But Farrakhan also enjoys a very large public following of non-Muslims who pack the halls whenever he lectures. He also commands a vast television audience, and on occasion he has enraged the Jewish leadership by remarks or opinions interpreted as anti-Semitic. Whenever this has occurred, Jewish leaders have immediately called on "respectable black leadership" to publicly repudiate Farrakhan under threat of Jewish disavowal of the long-strained rapprochement that once signified the black-Jewish alliance in the common struggle for civil rights.

This practice, however well intentioned, has generally exacerbated the raveling of relations between Jews and Blacks rather than relieving it, for the tangle of issues in question is far too complex for such simplistic remedies in these times of critical social and political restructuring. In this instance the problems begin with an uncertain definition of *anti-Semitism* and range all the way to the most effective means of dealing with it where it does in fact exist. Particularly unacceptable to African Americans has been the repeated spectacle of having respected black leaders "short-pantsed" in the media by Jewish leaders demanding instant denunciation of Farrakhan. Black leaders, whatever their private opinions about Mr. Farrakhan or his rhetoric, are emasculated and enraged by such public call-outs by their Jewish counterparts. They are too painfully reminiscent of the days when the black leadership was often frozen until "the word" came from the structures of power "downtown." Moreover, few African Americans are impressed by strategies of countering rhetoric with more rhetoric. They have heard too often "Look what we said" when what they longed to hear was "Look what we did" to put much faith in denunciatory rhetoric. Besides, it would seem to be obvious that Minister Farrakhan's power and influence do not depend on his popularity with Jews, or on a high approval rating from conventional African American leadership, which is often already suspected of being dependent and other-directed. Farrakhan's primary constituency is hard core, gut level, and anchored firmly in the black grass roots, who have not yet been heard from politically precisely because they neither trust nor respect a black leadership that may be susceptible to external manipulation. But the Muslim minister can also claim an undetermined spectrum of support outside his immediate community from followers who are intrigued by his approach to many economic and political issues that have nothing to do with religion. In October 1995 a million African American men marched on Washington at the behest of Louis Farrakhan, thus making moot forever the question of whether he could be effectively "delegitimized" through the rhetoric of denunciation by more "respectable" black leadership. In this huge bonding of black males, impressive numbers were from the black middle class, thus revealing the extraordinary reach of his message and charisma and making him a formidable stalking-horse for future political consideration.

In the final analysis, however, Louis Farrakhan is, for all the attention given him, as yet a relatively minor aspect of the social revolution implicit in new patterns of behavior springing up all over a world grown restive under the old formulas for the distribution of scarce resources. The world is changing, and America will change with it, whether Americans will or no. Indeed, the question is not whether we will change, but whether we will maximize the possibilities inherent in change for the realignment of our structures for the promotion of human dignity and social justice. Change in the form of shifting patterns of immigration and proselytization may have already displaced Judaism with Islam as the second major religion in America. If this does not suggest the magnitude of the change that is already here and how it may affect our racial dilemma, perhaps it is time to look again, and this time with eyes that see. Before World War II there was only a handful of minorities of statistical consequence in America. Today there are dozens—all clamoring for, and all entitled to, their fair share of the American Dream. Surely this has significance for what we learned yesterday in the black struggle for determination to overcome bias and privilege and preemption. Since the Civil Rights movement, that determination has produced a black governor, a senator, and hundreds of mayors and other elected officials throughout America. By 1994 there were at least forty African Americans in the Congress of the United States. America is a better place to live for all this. It could be better still—something worth remembering as the challenge of multiculture takes on the substance of reality.

V

SEARCH FOR IDENTITY: THE WHATNESS OF WHO

Three Hundred Fifty

  Years and More

Three Thousand Miles

  from the Afric shore

A new law

American!

A new language

American!

A new God

American!

A new name

American!

American . . .

But my face is Black.

—C. ERIC LINCOLN,

This Road since Freedom

I think it was Tacitus, one of the Seven Sages of ancient Greece, who laid it down that "what is, is, and nothing else is at all." An inarguable proposition, it would seem, however tautological, but when we extrapolate it to read "who is, is who he is, and no one else at all," we open up a Pandora's box of contradiction. In this society we are seldom who we are, and almost never who we think we are, because *who* is defined by *what,* and *what* is a construct of race and place.

Human identity comes in three possible perspectives of reality: personal, conventional, and abstract. Only abstract identity— the sum of physical and psychological, spiritual, emotional, and moral attributes annealed in the sum of experience—can be reckoned one's true or absolute identity; that is, the true self presumed to interact with other selves similarly constituted in the interface of human experience. But like beauty and art, identity is also a persistent image in the eye of the beholder. When that prevailing image is "public" and at great variance with one's self-perception, a kind of negotiated identity without necessary reference to the *real* becomes the identity of record, the self to be recognized in ordinary social intercourse. It is the identity of record (IR) by which black people are generally known in their constant interface with their white counterparts in America. This IR is not necessarily a mean ground between extremes of perception. Rather, it is the most convenient and effective recognition available from the brokers who set the terms for political and social engagement. It is the market price for recognition in the human scheme of values. There is always another self behind the mask of blackness which shuts out the possibility of a more favorable perception. The degree to which that other self may affirm or negate the identity of record will vary in direct proportion to the degree of security and self-confidence defining the environment of social engagement. Such environments range all the way from those which produce absolute black anonymity, as in Ralph Ellison's *Invisible Man,* to extreme, highly focused visibility, as in the case of black media idol O. J. Simpson, who was accused of murdering his white ex-wife. Sometimes the sense of white security, or the lack of it, reflects in pejorative perceptions of selective subclasses of invisible people such as young black males, Black Muslims, or others whose mere existence seems to be threatening. Hence, for most black people the identity that emerges is the identity that is politically permissible, a statement long implied in the X of Malcolm X, which alluded to a more fundamental identity not yet permitted to surface. The IR is at minimum the identity that is consistent with the perceived requirements of survival. True identity is the identity of self-perception in search of creative social intercourse with other selves in an environment of mutual respect and receptivity.

Every black American knows firsthand the slander of invisibility. Anonymity. It comes in a thousand ways: a word, a gesture, a conversation that moves over and around him as though he or she were not present. Invisibility is most painful when it is preclusive—jobs not offered, invitations not issued, opportunities denied. It is a lifelong incubus from which few if any African Americans ever escape completely, no matter what their attainments. Racial anonymity derives from the presumption of inconsequence—the inconsequence of black persons and of their achievements, actual or potential. Their strivings, their struggles, their attainments are simply not counted—by consensus—like the ballots cast by Blacks in the political elections of the South for decades after Reconstruction. The feeling of anonymity is the weird sense of not being where you know you are; a game of hide-and-seek in which you don't have to go anywhere not to be found. A case in point: I had been at Duke University for several years when one of the deans decided to honor the dozen or so Fellows of the American Academy of Arts and Sciences teaching at the university at that time. Accordingly, a lavish dinner was booked, invitations were mailed, and Steven Grabaud, secretary of the American Academy, arrived to address the Fellows and to congratulate the university on its fledgling representation. As it turned out, the first thing asked of the distinguished gathering was "Where is C. Eric Lincoln?" I was not present, as I had not been invited, but I am told that the academic faces were as red as the lobsters on which they dined. The dean probably had the reddest face of all, or she should have, for I had been a Fellow of the Academy for several years and was an occasional contributor to *Daedalus,* its scholarly journal, all of which was a matter of record in the university files which were reviewed annually, by her office. But racial presumption never sleeps, and the operating presumption had been that my anonymity was justified. *I didn't count, so I was not counted.* Accordingly I missed the lavish dinner with the more visible fellow Fellows of the American Academy at Duke University. But, not to worry, the situation could be retrieved (and my anonymity reestablished) through a dinner of chicken pickin's with the Kentucky Colonel with the black string tie, who featured standard fare for invisible folks like me.

In 1995 Lawrence Wilder, black former governor of Virginia, was "roughed up" by an impatient security guard at the Raleigh-Durham airport in North Carolina. Although the governor is known widely for his courtliness, the white security guard, with his instincts tuned to a set of social perceptions which predefined all black men, could not imagine that the well-dressed, urbane black man transiting his security station could be a person of any significance.

THE NAME IN THE GAME OF BLACK IDENTITY

Since the conventional understanding of identity is not fixed and unambiguous, who you are in the conventional mind may be determined in part by your place of origin; your principal associates; your ethnic or tribal name; your personal or family name; your intimate name, or nickname; your principal employment; your religion; your residence; your color; your speech patterns; or some or all of these, and more. *Who* is often a mosaic of minibits of *what,* and when that mosaic becomes too complex or too inconvenient for schedules of prejudgment already in place, the shorthand of conventional perception takes over: an identity is thrust upon you. A name is not an identity, of course, but it may be designed to function as an informal window on identity. In the rural South where I grew up, nicknames were common and were usually relied upon as a kind of introductory index of personality, description, or behavior. Some were colorful: Big Walkin' Man, Snout, Ug, Do Funny, Tootie Fruity, Shab, Mallet Foot, Guts. Some were practical means of sorting out and giving personal identity to related or closely associated individuals in the extended families which were the norm in that time and place: Big Lucy, Little Lucy, Mama Lucy, Big Daddy, Big Mama, Old Tom, Son Tom. Some were less than complimentary: Jackleg, Low-life, Snake, Bubble Head, etc.

Names also function to relate identity to causes, movements, religions, and other matters which may be considered of critical import to the individual or the group with which that person is commonly identified. In unusual cases names may represent an inverse or confused relationship to a pejorative identity. For example, a hundred years after the Civil War, one of the most popular names for black males in the South was Robert Lee. For every black Ulysses Grant drafted in World War II, there was probably a score of black Robert Lees to fight beside him.

Names are symbols of convenience, and not paradigms of substance; but they do refer to real entities, and because they do, they take on consociational significance which becomes a critical element in the construct of identity. In the conventional mind, for example, if "nigger," "peckerwood," and "Dago" are words repeatedly linked with identifiable human types, the initial awareness that distinguishes the appellation from its subject is likely to diminish with repetitive experience, and in time the two may become so interlinked as to require a considerable conscious effort to realize that the name is not the person. This is a syndrome so commonly experienced by African Americans as to produce a continuing anxiety regarding group identity, or "a name to go by." The long and painful odyssey from African to Negro to person of color to colored to Black to Afro-American to African American is well known, as are the more deliberately disparaging appellations "nigger," "darkie," "coon," and the like. But whatever their intent, the suspicion that the conventional perceptions of white people end up in pejorative refraction induced a black anxiety which verged on paranoia and was promptly added to the black catalog of deficits. How can a group of people who can't even agree on who they are, *even after they have been told,* be expected to ever agree on anything of substance like self-direction! The impact of the "multiculturalism" (whatever that turns out to be) that is reshaping America will be considerably less jarring the more we know about the inner linings of constituent cultures and how they arrived at the peculiar impasses which delay their full participation in the common ventures of the society they now share with so many others of differentiated ethnic or cultural experience. For African Americans, a comprehensive accounting undoubtedly lies ahead in the self-determined blossoming literature of the African American experience, despite the strange reluctance of American academe to learn any more than it is presumed to know already about its oldest, biggest, and potentially most productive minority.

OUT OF AFRICA

It is a bitter lesson in the classic ironies which mark the trail of human history to have to remember that it all began in America's insatiable demand for labor. Black labor. It is ironic because the demand for black labor is not so insatiable now. As a matter of fact, literally millions of young black men, once the top of the market for American labor, are bypassed when America goes shopping for its labor needs today. Maybe it's because their labor isn't pro bono anymore. But it is hard not to remember those other times when Indian slavery was tried and proved impractical because the Indians disappeared into their own forests, and when European "indenture" was tried and abandoned because the Europeans could not be held beyond seven years and expected a stake toward self-sufficiency upon completion of their terms. It was to the involuntary African immigrant that America turned to supply the labor to build an empire. Free. The supply of Africans was inexhaustible, it seemed, and they did not enjoy the protection of familiar forests, as did the Indians, or of the British Crown, as did the indentured servants. The Africans were without any recourse whatever, except for the enormous dependency their free labor engendered.

It is variously estimated that during the centuries-long era of African slavery in the New World, somewhere between twelve and thirty million Africans were forcibly torn from the routine of settled life in African towns and villages and involuntarily resettled as chattels in America. No one will ever know the exact number, of course, because the business of human bondage did not run to strict accounting of the silent percentages which for one reason or another were lost to the slave entrepreneurs between the capture and the delivery of the human commodities being traded. However, a reasonable estimate based on the numbers finally delivered to the slave markets in the New World suggests that the involuntary West African diaspora fed into the funnel of capture, chattelization, transport, and redistribution that history has labeled "the rape of Africa" must have been sufficiently massive to leave that continent struggling in the trauma of demoralization and cultural shock for centuries.

The depersonalization of the African that was to reach its perfection in America began in West Africa. The repugnance and indignity of the public slave coffles, the humiliation and the status stripping of the undifferentiated herding of hostile strangers of conflicting cultures and ideologies into the factories or barracoons, and the abject dehumanization of the death ships of the "middle passage" were all preparatory to the terrible finale played out in the rice swamps of South Carolina, the tobacco fields of Virginia, and the vast cotton plantations of Georgia, Alabama, Mississippi, and Louisiana. On the auction block the last claims on human respectability would be denied, and at the fall of the gavel, identity—personal and corporate—would be forever consigned to the indiscriminate oblivion of slavery. Only spiritual identity remained. *Anybody who was a child of God could never be nobody,* and on that slender filament of faith the reconstruction of the African American sense of self would ultimately depend.

As we must look to America to find the roots of the process which stripped the African American of identity, so must we look to Africa for the primary sources of its restoration. Critical to this task is some understanding of the West African religious cosmos out of which came the vast majority of the African forebears whose life and labor constitute the primary cultural base of contemporary African American existence. No detailed analysis is possible here, of course, but the principles I cite are commonly agreed upon by all those who retain a kinship with their origins. Traditional West African religion allows for one supreme or High God, the creator of humankind. Man is not the end product of an evolutionary process, but came into existence through a deliberate act of his maker. At a minimum, man is body, mind, and spirit, which together constitute his humanity. The body is susceptible to destruction and decay. Mind is an innate quality of moral discrimination unique to the human species, and the spirit is either divine essence or has certain critical offices or responsibilities in the divine scheme of things. A sustained or meaningful relationship with God is patently impossible if mind and spiritual identity, which together constitute the principal index of human accountability, are confused or ignored. As a matter of fact, from the African understanding of religious priorities, the confusion of identity in the world of the living must of necessity reverberate in the world where the spirits of the departed continue their existence after death, for there is no disjunction between these two worlds, which represent different but interrelated aspects of reality.

The spirit world is an aspect of the physical world, and the spirits which inhabit it are principally ancestral, which is to say, they are the abiding manifestations of the primogeniture to which the living owe their existence. More than that, they are ever present, or they can be summoned by the living for advice and counsel and other forms of support in times of crisis, or in times of celebration. So long as the name of the departed ancestor is remembered or called upon, so long will his or her spirit be available to champion the interests of the individual, the family, the community or the clan of which it was (and remains) a member.

But the ancestral spirits have an even more critical role. While the God of traditional West African religion cares about man as his superlative creation, the Western notion of God as immanent or ever present is not a prominent feature of the God-man relationship. African myths and cosmogonies abound which account for God's distancing himself from the human community, even though he cares about it. Here the ever-present ancestral spirits perform a crucial service as intermediaries between God, the lesser divinities, and the human individual or community. In times of anxiety or distress they can be called upon to intercede with the Supreme High God, who lives beyond direct human experience but is immediately available through these ancestral emissaries.

Despite the apparent orderliness of procedure, the world of spirits is not necessarily irenic, but rather the invisible counterpart of the more familiar world of human passions and behaviors. The ancestral spirits contend and compete with other spirits and with each other for power and influence and approbation. Individual spirits may be benign, evil, or indifferent, but the ancestral spirits are characteristically protective of their own living counterparts, and it is here that precise identity takes on compelling significance. The identity of the clan, the tribe, the family, the individual ward, or the petitioner must be established beyond any doubt before the ancestral spirits can be successfully invoked. Hence tribal names, family names, personal names, and day names converge in an interlocking system of precise identification. The African individual is always *more* than merely an individual: he or she is always located within an expanding system of relationships which ultimately link them to God. If that system breaks down or is ruptured at any point, the African's sense of identity is lost, and with it the sense of nexus or proper belonging. A Malawan proverb puts it this way: "A man is a man because of others. Life is when you are together, alone you are an animal." It is these interlocking linkages between individual, clan, tribe, and family, including ancestral spirits, that pose such formidable cultural barriers between Africans in Africa and Africans of the diaspora. The sentiments for conciliation and common cause may all be present, but the problem of "identifying" the expatriate and relocating him or her in the proper niche in the African cosmos is an uncertain adventure in frustration. African life is never casual or arbitrary; and identity is the primary key to inclusion and participation in that life.

FACELESSNESS

By the time the African slaves arrived in America, their identities had already been substantially blurred, and nothing in the experience ahead held any promise of relief. Woloff and Fulani, Yoruba and Fanti, Mandingo and Ibo, Whydah and Ashanti; Muslim, naturist, warrior, sorcerer, priestess, herdsman, chief, prince, diviner, sage, and woodcarver were all cast into the common cauldron of facelessness and denigration that American slavery required. History was suspended, and that part out of which all status and all relationships derive, and which constitutes the only sure reality in African cosmology, was summarily denied or leached away. American slavery offered "no place to be somebody" and less opportunity to know the difference.

But it took time for this malicious syndrome to perfect itself, and the abject slave mentality it was designed to produce never did become absolute. Whatever the merits of the arguments and counterarguments about the retention of African culture by the African Americans of the diaspora, suffice it to say that the Africans who came to America still called themselves African long after the slavocracy had supposedly accomplished its goals of a perfect cultural tabula rasa for its chattels, and long after the particularities of African identity had been lost in the process of reduction and homogenization. There remained to haunt the involuntary expatriates a residual awareness, the retention of an alter image of something that once had been that needs must be again. However, the religious modalities of West Africa which had been so critical to the African's sense of style and place could not be replicated in America. The evolving policies of slave management required the summary dispersal of slaves from the same tribe or those speaking the same language as a precaution against insurrection. Furthermore, slave gatherings for purposes of religious worship were routinely forbidden as paganistic or as time stolen from the master. The drum, the essential instrument in

African worship, was forbidden; and slaves caught participating in African religious rituals of any kind were flogged, branded, or sold. No substantive efforts to include the African slaves in the religious life of America occurred until 1701, when the Society for the Propagation of the Gospel in Foreign Parts (SPG), the missionary arm of the Anglican church, petitioned the planters to permit them to exhort selected slaves gathered on the "big house" commons. This was almost a hundred years after the first interface between Englishmen and Africans in America took place at Jamestown, Virginia, in 1619. In the meantime, slave identity was a secondary derivative of ownership: "Mr. Whitley's Jim" or "Miss Tillie's Zenia." Racial identity was no longer a question to be addressed, for the "peculiar institution" had long since become a black institution: every African was presumed to be a slave, and every slave was presumed to be of African derivation. Thus the erstwhile Africans had a presumptive identity thrust upon them while they struggled for self-definition. The enslavement of Indians and the indenture of Europeans were relegated to a past America felt no need to remember, and "slave" and "African" became synonymous categories. Still the Africans clung to the only identity that made sense to them, despite the slow erosion of the values it once represented. In the evolving culture of the plantation, the "lying Africans," "thieving Africans," and "malingering Africans" perceived from the perspectives of the big house gradually found their pejorative counterparts in such labels as "ol' African," "ugly African," and "black African" that black children learned to use in denigration of each other, so deeply had the psychology of racial denigration seeped into and corrupted the cultural infrastructure of its victims. Long, long, long before *Brown* v. *Board of Education* in 1954, the African dolls were ugly by African American standards, and white dolls were the ones of preferred identity. As the external slave trade gradually diminished and the introduction of freshly caught Africans abated, the once proud Africans were increasingly defined, and frequently defined themselves, by other appellations. Their personal names were usually determined by the master, or by his policy or decree, and their only corporate identity was that of "darkies," "Negroes," "colored," or other pejorative assignations designed to identify Africans as a genre without granting them recognition as individuals.

The simplistic rendering of identity would be modified somewhat, at least internally, by the eventual development of black religion as the primary institutionalization of the corporate schedule of values peculiar to African interests in America. After protracted resistance to the pleas of the SPG that its missionaries be granted access to the heathen souls of the benighted Africans on the plantations, the planters finally relented. They succumbed to the arguments that conversion would in no case work manumission (causing them to forfeit their property to Christ), and that Christianized slaves were safer, more reliable, and less troublesome than the "raw heathens" who came out of the African bush. In due course the missionaries and other exhorters were permitted on the plantations, carefully watched by the planters, preaching mostly to the big house retainers gathered under the magnolias on an occasional Sunday afternoon. The spiritual message of this "magnolia mission" was not one calculated to stir any feelings of discontent with the life of bondage, or any longing for an identity that used to be. Rather, the existing confusion of identity was reenforced by making the slaves understand that cursed by God, they and their descendants were forever destined to be "hewers of wood and drawers of water" under the gratuitous oversight of the white Christians God himself had appointed to be their wardens.

In time the most intimate retainers of the big house compound—the nannies, body servants, grooms, dressmakers, and such—would be permitted to attend the white man's church with their masters and mistresses. Dressed in the discarded finery of the big house, they were assigned segregated benches placed for their use along the walls or in the rear of the church. When their numbers increased beyond this convenience, some churches built galleries for their Negro members up under the rafters of the sanctuary. Inevitably, these spiritual aeries came to be known colloquially as "nigger heavens," and are so known today.

Perhaps this was progress of a sort—from the magnolia missions on the big house compound to the cathedral heights of the master's church; but in the eyes of the world they knew most intimately, Africans in America were still Negroes, darkies, *niggers*—without so much as a name of their own to anchor them to any reality they cared about, or wanted to be a part of.

It is clear from the black experience in the white church that identity is not a fixed value to be arbitrarily conferred or inferred from principles of reason or rationality. In classical Islam, for example, religious values eclipse all others and unite believers in one universal *umma,* or brotherhood, transcending race, class, and nationality. In the West, and more particularly in the United States, it is racial rather than religious identity that represents superlative human value, thus fixing forever the conditions of individual acceptance, and participation in the ongoing human cavalcade. In consequence, the African American struggle for identity has always been in the face of established convention that precluded a priori any investiture of commonality in religion. To put it less delicately, in America, Christian identity alone and of itself has never been of sufficient moment to open any doors of consequence. The established criteria for superlative acceptability require that one be both Christian *and* white, with race being the constant value in the equation. Merely to be Christian is not enough; yet, as we shall see, it was precisely on religion that African American identity ultimately staked its claim for recognition.

In the meantime, all of the laws, customs, conventions, and taboos which functioned together to preclude a negotiable identity for any person of any degree of African descent whatever flew in the face of logic, even as they now scramble before the uncompromising revelations of modern genetic investigation.

There probably has not been a "pure" African born in America to native African Americans for a hundred years, for the universal tendency of the human species to mix and mingle despite all disclaimers has left America with a numerous and historic progeny, which if law and convention count for truth, are altogether imaginary since they are neither white nor black. Imagination needs no identity, but people are not people without one.

THE PROBLEM OF DUALITY

Despite its specious appeal as the instant solution to a persistent problem, the African American struggle for identity has not been a struggle to be white, but rather to enjoy parity and equivalence in being human. While tens of thousands of African Americans have found it expedient to "pass" (for white) in pursuit of common values precluded by black identity, the larger numbers who have the capacity to pass but have preferred not to do so would seem to be evidence of the fact that true identity is a value beyond expediency, and that those who prefer to pass are tautologically passing for what they are already. In short, passing in the search for identity almost always implies an act of expedience rather than an estimate of value. This would seem to suggest that the childhood experience of strong identification with the white doll (as in Dr. Kenneth Clark's demonstration in the *Brown* case) is modified or corrected by the time options are matched with age and experience. Hence the critical question for African Americans has always been not how to assume an existing identity which "works" for the majority, but how to fashion a "new" identity out of a new experience in a new environment and have it accepted for what it is.

Scholar-philosopher W. E. B. Du Bois grappled with this problem in his famous soliloquy on double consciousness as "two souls, two thoughts, two unreconciled strivings, two warring ideals in one dark body."[1] But Du Bois's inner turmoil was essentially intellectual—a clash of the rational refinements produced by the most prominent citadels of reason available to him with the abject suppression of that same reason beyond the narrow parameters of his mind. Hence the Du Boisian dubiety was a confusion of reason and experience, a contradiction that was to haunt Du Bois throughout his long life.

But W. E. B. Du Bois was not *black every-person,* and his peculiar set of personal circumstances did not equip him to be the

1. W. E. B. Du Bois, *The Souls of Black Folk* (1903), Fisk Diamond Jubilee edition (Nashville: Fisk University Press, 1979), p. 17.

archetypical expression of the black experience. Born free of mixed parentage in Massachusetts and educated at Fisk, Harvard, and Heidelburg, W. E. B. Du Bois was certainly a "Negro" by prevailing American sentiments (with all the pejoration that term implied), but by virtue of his unique set of personal circumstances he was not totally confined by the implications of that appellation. Nor is there any reason to assume his abject accommodation to the role he is so frequently called on to dramatize for all other African Americans. While Du Bois's search for identity was essentially a personal intellectual enterprise in self-clarification, the struggle of the black masses to achieve identity has been a gut struggle in the pursuit of group recognition and dignification. When it became clear that the white man's Christianity could not or would not afford the inclusive cover human dignity required, it was obvious that some other modus vivendi would have to be discovered or invented. But except for the church, slavery provided no institutional opportunities even remotely available to black dignification, and the prevailing image of the church was of a white institution substantially accommodated to black debasement.

CHURCH AND IDENTITY

But there was an alternative church, an "underground church," dubbed by history "the invisible institution." It was a *black* church that developed outside of and independently of the white man's church that would ultimately give definition to the individual black person and would become a powerful force in the reclamation of personal identity. The invisible black church was totally African, and it met clandestinely in the deep woods and thickets, as far removed from the white man's sight and sensitivities as could be managed. This invisible institution was the church of the field hands who could not be accommodated with the favored big house retainers in the galleries of the white churches, although it was often led by black preachers who had learned something of the Bible in the white churches or from hearing the scripture read to the retainers of the big house. But in the outdoor tabernacle of the swamps, the sandhills, and the backwoods, the ambience was different. The music, the prayers, and the testimonials were rooted in the day-to-day experiences of plantation life, and the prevailing message was not "obey your masters," but *"God wants you . . . free!"* To be *wanted* was a powerful, unaccustomed affirmation of self-estimate. To be wanted *free,* like other people, could only mean that God wanted them to be responsible—to him, for where there is no freedom the notion of responsibility is a mockery. True identity, the unfettered projection of the self, is the inalienable corollary of freedom, if not indeed its first function. Identity is the projection of somebodyness, the sum of a differentiated, individuated human being. A *person.* But despite the spiritual subliminals of the invisible church, freedom was not yet, and personal identity remained contingent to God's waiting time. But the sense of impending liberation was unmistakable. A traditional black spiritual of the period spelled it out:

> *If anybody asks you*
> *Who I am*
> *Who I am*
> *Who I am*
> *If anybody asks you*
> *Who I am*
> *You can tell 'em*
> *I'm a child of God!*

Identity enough. But not for this life.

Despite the general policy of suppressing black religion, by the last quarter of the eighteenth century, a number of small black Baptist churches had been allowed to develop along the eastern seaboard, particularly in Virginia, South Carolina, and Georgia. These "independent" black churches were always under the oversight of white men, for religious gatherings were prohibited by law except in the presence of specified numbers of white monitors. Nevertheless, these black congregations represented the only institutionalized constituencies available to black initiative, and they immediately became the popular reference of individual identification. While the big house slaves in their masters' churches had also called themselves Methodist or Baptist, or occasionally Presbyterian, not until the coming of the independent black churches did "church identity" take on the essence of nationality and personal evolution. The anonymity resulting from the ruthless homogenizing of race and place in the creation of the slave caste was finally relieved to some degree. If one could no longer define oneself as Ashanti or Yoruba, the identity as Baptist or Methodist conveyed some notion, however minimal, of who one perceived oneself to be. Nat Turner's religiously inspired assault on slavery in 1831 is said to have been launched with his explicit instructions that "the people called Methodist" were not to be harmed, suggesting that religious denomination as an index of identity was by then well established in the African mind, and that to the African, it transcended race and place. Even to this day in parts of the rural South some settlements or communities still take their primary identification from church affiliation.

For those in the developing African American subculture, church identity was consistent with their perception of their larger identity as children of God. The first black denomination was chartered in 1815, and the black churches began a rapid and truly independent development during (and following) the Civil War. The fact that there was a distinctive African presence in the Bible contributed to the sense that Africans, too, were clearly identified as "People of God," an identity stretching back to the portals of human history. Hence the African American sojourn in slavery, like that of the Jews in Egypt, was a transitory experience, but the Africa of the biblical experience was there from the beginning of things and would be there at the end. Accordingly, the reclamation of African identity underscored the ancient relationship with God, and it became the imprimatur of record symbolized in the names of the earliest black churches: First African Baptist in Savannah (1788), Abyssinian Baptist in New York (1808), the First African Episcopal Church of St. Thomas, and Bethel African Methodist Episcopal Church, the latter two founded in Philadelphia in 1794 as the progeny of the Free African Society, the first self-consciously black organization in America. The first two black denominations, the African Methodist Episcopal Church (1815) and the African Methodist Episcopal Zion Church (1820), were both "African" communions.[2] The message of challenge offered by the evangelists and exhorters, Methodist and Baptist alike, who followed the Union armies south was: "Sheep and goats are not of a kind. Come out from among those who demean you and join onto your own! Be African!" And they came out, by the tens of thousands, for the black church was now the undisputed nexus of the emergent black experience, and "African" was the identity of choice.

Religion is not nationality, of course, but it is often made to function as if it were when nationality has been clouded or put in doubt. In the African American experience, in which every critical index of cultural and personal identity had been ridiculed, forbidden, suppressed, or denied, religion became the closest approximation of African corporate identity—not because all African religious beliefs were the same, but because belief and practice in America had become sufficiently common to the African American subculture to provide a framework of reference from which a common identity could reasonably be inferred. Significantly, it was *not* a reference sufficiently common to black Christians and white Christians to transcend the race-rooted schedule of values and behaviors which still alienates black and white Christians from each other. But in spite of that unfortunate anomaly, the black church became African Americans' chief index of identification, because in every critical sense it was the one satisfactory projection of themselves that found least resistance from the significant others upon which its viability would ultimately depend.

It must be clear by now that the metaphysics of identity in the context of race and place is not so simple. The African Americans salvaged an intuitive appreciation of their African heritage from an antecedent culture rooted in the world of ancestral African spirits, and from the African presence proclaimed and documented in the Sacred Book common to all Christian witness. Their faithfulness to that identity was boldly and vigorously attested in the designation of the earliest black societies, churches,

2. C. Eric Lincoln and Lawrence H. Mamiya, *The Black Church in the African American Experience* (Durham: Duke University Press, 1990), pp. 47ff.

denominations, and distinctive rituals as "African," in a deter-mined effort to mandate and project a prideful affirmative con-scious of themselves as a people of consequence with a destiny beyond the reckoning of the travail of the moment. If God lives, the wheel must turn.

Identity may be intensely personal, but in its practical expres-sion it is not solely a personal determination, and therein lies the answer to the persistent problem of *who* for the African American individual or generic. "A name to go by" is the symbol by which identity is labeled or signified, but the symbol is functional only to the degree that it is capable of initiating a response from sig-nificant others that is reasonably or contractually consistent with its intended signification. Self-perception is prime grist for the mills of social refraction, and identity is in limbo until there is at least a working consensus on what comes from between the rollers. Where social or political power is the determining fac-tor, a working identity of sorts, the identity of record, may be created by fiat. But to the degree that the power which sustains that fiat compromises or violates for whatever reason the identity of self-perception, there will always be a struggle to redress the balance.

The issue of identity may appear trivial at times to those un-affected by its negative connotations. For example, there is strong resistance in the print media to spelling *black* with an uppercase B when it is used as a proper noun to signify ethnic or cultural identity. But there is no such resistance in the case of White Rus-sian, South Dakotan, West Virginian, Blackfoot Indians, or Green Berets, or other instances in which common nouns may also func-tion as proper nouns. Such paranoia suggests that in the dark cor-ners of the human psyche there still lurks the suspicion that the name and what it symbolizes are one and the same, or that there is a direct power relationship between the name and the person who "owns" it. The inability of prejudiced persons to differentiate the subjects of their disdain or to "remember" their names, and their reluctance to accord them ordinary titles of civil respect are legendary. And though the syndrome still persists, it may well be rooted in a forgotten age when the independent power of words to curse, to damn, to bless, or to endow was taken for granted. A name is indeed something more than the sum of its letters; it is a statement about identity, and identity is the mystique of human essence which in the conventional mind may represent a repository of power, the expression of which must be carefully negotiated or regulated in the interests of public policy lest it disturb the prevailing social equilibrium. For example, in the early days of World War II, the state of North Carolina allegedly refused to grant a birth certificate to a child christened "Tojo Hitler," even though that bilious apothegm broke no law and lay within the presumptive rights of the parents and the limitations of free speech.

The African American predicament is still in search of a solution which will permit a whole subculture to get past the crepe of blackness for a more realistic and uninhibited participation in the common experience of being American. We long for some miracle of illumination that will give transparency to the packaging of color and all the depressing ideologies which rest upon it. The somber history of peremptory rejection in the persistence of notions of race and place as immutable categories has been a long and uncertain search for an identity surreptitiously declared missing, but which in reality was always there in place for the sober minded to see, to recognize, and to engage. We have yet to concede that whatever the race and place, the *what* and *who* are always the same. A rose by any other name is still a rose, and not a carnation—or a ragweed.

VI

HUMAN VALUES AND INHUMAN SYSTEMS

America

You were my teacher

In the statement of your law

I looked for Justice

in the dogma of your faith

I searched for mercy.

—C. ERIC LINCOLN,

This Road since Freedom

The search for identity is meaningless unless that identity is confirmed as an existence of consequence by the prevailing spectrum of values by which it is measured. *What difference does it make?* That is the crux of the issue. Our values constitute the contextual framework out of which our more critical decisions are made and our volitional behavior is determined. Some behavioral psychologists would probably object to this assessment because the rats and pigeons they study suggest that all significant behavior is but a patterned response to external stimuli. But most people are not pigeons, and fewer still are rats, our occasional similarities of behavior notwithstanding. Rats have instincts, but people have codes of proscriptive and prescriptive reference governing their behavior. These "values" are the motivational determiners of what we will or will not do. One way to test the importance of human values is to review the very broad spectrum of social changes that have occurred in our society since World War II. Advances in technology, medicine, ecology, and other fields have often prompted the reformation of structures of value to permit, sanitize, or sanctify new behaviors (and some not so new) which derive from broadened perceptions of human possibility, or human fragility, as the case may be. In consequence, it is increasingly difficult for people to retain a strong sense of moral security and to maintain confidence in their perceptions of what is right, or even whether right or wrong makes any difference. Mental depression is endemic as more and more people struggle to sort out and make sense of the competing notions and experiences which seem to crowd in upon us. Our values, particularly those based on religious understanding, have always functioned as stations of security in a world where all else is in flux. And because we have held them to be primal and immutable, those values expressing the creativity of God and the dignity of man become even more critical to meaning and direction in human life. Some things must change; but some things must persist through change, or change itself becomes the only value of significance. How a society deals with change in the context of those fundamental values which do not change is the measure of its vitality and the prognosis of its future.

THE CARDINAL VALUES

There are some values which must be fundamental to every civilized society, and from these, other values may be derived. The fundamental values include life, dignity, creativity, and responsibility. Life, because it is the ground and the condition for all else. Where there is no life there is no possibility. To have life, to sustain life, to conserve life is to affirm the creative genius of the Divine and to participate in the divine scheme at the highest level. I know of no moral sentiment superior to that which values life above all else, and which finds in that valuation the sanctions by which all behavior is ultimately to be determined.

Where life is not the superlative value, no culture can preserve itself, for the appreciation of life begets life, protects life, nurtures and enhances life. And life in turn writes on the tabula rasa of the material world the purpose for which all that is has come into existence. But life is not all there is to it, and I make no apologies to Shakespeare or convention when I say, "To be, or not to be, is but *part* of the question." For not merely to be, but to be *with dignity* is part of the first condition of being human. Dignity is the inalienable corollary of human life, and the affirmation of life is the confirmation of life with dignity. If, as Plato suggested, the unexamined life is not worth living, it is no less true that the life that is bereft of the elemental symbols of human recognition is a negation of divine purpose and intent, and a mockery of what the term *humanity* is intended to signify. Mere existence may satisfy the primary definition of a frog, a lizard, or a sand fly, but to be with dignity is the minimum condition of being human.

To be human and to be so considered, that is the meaning of dignity. Dignity means to be able to live and to move among one's fellows clothed with all those symbols, tangible and intangible, which convey to the self and to all others that one's being is a matter of consequence, not a mere quivering in the infinity of time and space. But dignity implies *creativity*, endowment with human genius. It assumes the organization and projection of those peculiar attributes which allow the "whoness" and the "whatness" of living some expression of personal significance beyond the satisfaction of the requirements of survival. The true measure of the significance of human existence is that it is endowed with possibilities beyond itself. It is capable of bringing something new into being. Every human being is capable of projecting the imprimatur of the self upon the backdrop of history, so that when his or her summons comes to join "that innumerable inevitable caravan," death need hold no terrors deriving from the conclusion of a life of inanity. Creativity is the indisputable evidence that one has indeed experienced life, the only ground for any other possible experience, and that one has added one's signature of affirmation to that most extraordinary privilege that God, and God only, can bestow. As life is the supreme product of the divine will, so must creativity be the unimpaired option of every human life. Verily, "a life is a terrible thing to waste," and where the creative potential inherent in human existence is stifled or permitted to atrophy for want of nurture or opportunity, a society is a contradiction in terms, feeding on its own progeny.

Finally, life implies, indeed it requires *responsibility*, for responsibility is the minimum condition for meaningful participation in the social enterprise. When men and women choose to live in cooperation with each other in pursuit of that spectrum of common values not available to them as individuals, such an arrangement can be viable only to the degree that all parties are capable of responding adequately to the requirements of that mutual undertaking. But responsibility requires the ability to *respond*, and where this ability has been impaired or held back from selected individuals or classes, by whatever means and for whatever reasons, those so deprived are robbed of a vital element of human consideration. Their impairment conditions every aspect of their participation in the common ventures of the human enterprise, and they can never be responsible if they never have the means to be responsible. *If you break the beagle's back, he can't run rabbits with the rabbit pack!* And if the ability to run rabbits is the primary criterion by which a beagle's worth is determined, so is the ability to respond in kind to the criteria of human valuation. *Responsibility presumes the means to be responsible.* To be human is to be confirmed in the possession of those minimum facilities which make responsible participation possible in the ordinary spectrum of human affairs.

These, then, are very fundamental human values: *life itself* and its inalienable corollaries: *dignity, creativity,* and *responsibility.* For those of us in the Judeo-Christian tradition who perceive humankind in the image of God, these are the critical elements of that perception. But religion aside, every human individual is at a minimum the counterpart of every other human individual, and the brutalization of one implies the susceptibility of all. If being human has any significance whatever, it must by definition include the assurance that the symbols by which humanity is defined and distinguished cannot be arbitrarily ignored or discounted. In short, human life requires and must always be accorded conditions of existence commensurate with its superlative position in relation to all other possible values. In the absence of life, all else is academic; and in the absence of life's critical refinements, there can be neither meaning nor measure to mere abject human existence. For it is through these embellishments that the larger spectrum of values—including love, peace, justice, and tranquillity—find expression and enhancement in the human enterprise.

The values of which I speak are all "normative" to the culture, and they are all a part of the moral portfolio of the typical American. They are prominent in our religious creeds, encapsulated in the schoolday lore of our children, and enshrined in the fundamental legal principles which structure our understanding of America and what it means to be American. But they are also values which are commonly negated in practice through the covert systems of antivalues by means of which we protect the privileges and prerogatives of some through the blatant devaluation of others. It is this disjunction between what we will to believe and what we will to do that constitutes the continuing American dilemma, that persistent hypocrisy of values which enervates and qualifies our national life and makes us a nation of cynics.

THE PROBLEM OF THE COLOR LINE

The presumption of *race* is the basis of the contradiction that turns America against itself and issues in the compulsive mass negation of the critical values by which we claim to live. It was W. E. B. Du Bois's unerring appraisal almost a century ago that gave us a somber prediction of what to expect:

> The problem of the Twentieth Century is the problem of the color-line. . . .
>
> The Nation has not yet found peace from its sins. . . .[1]

His appraisal invited the troublesome conclusion that the race problem would never be solved until men learned to apply in dealings with their fellows the simple principles of the Golden Rule.

A lot of time has passed, and we still have not found peace from our sins; nor is the evidence that we entertain a serious commitment to the principles of the Golden Rule one of the compelling features of our generation. Prominent among our problems remains the perennial problem Du Bois complained of when the twentieth century was still in its infancy. That problem persists, despite the cynical snobbery of "political correctness" and the gossamer cosmetics of countless jerry-built "political solutions," and despite the hard-eyed reformers who promise the people change and then change the subject. The tortured strategies of those good, solid Americans whose consciences are always agonized but whose conveniences are rooted firmly in the status quo ante all come to nothing. It is still a problem of the color line, and that problem ramifies in all of our more critical relations,

1. *The Souls of Black Folk*, pp. 44, 19.

polluting the social environment and straining the parameters of credibility in which the democratic ideal is somehow expected to function. Wherever important human interests happen to lie, there the problem seems to lurk. It is not, as is so often urged by simplistic thinking, merely a matter of economics, for in America economics, like race, functions in the first rank of determination for access or denial to most scarce resources or opportunities. And when race and economics are so conjoined that one implies the other, millions of bona fide Americans find their chances of participation in the common ventures of America reduced to nothing palpable at all. They have the right without the right-of-way, which is to say that they have no available means of going where they have a *right* to go or the *will* to go. As far as meaningful participation in America is concerned, they are functionally disqualified. Shut out. A people thus handicapped cannot reasonably be asked to compete with those who are free of such impediments no matter *who* is or is not responsible for their impairment. The first order of business in a highway accident is not to quibble over who was at fault, but to take care of the casualties and get the road cleared so that the flow of traffic may resume. Everybody is at fault so long as anybody is excluded from the full enjoyment of his or her inalienable rights as a citizen and as a human being. Everybody is at fault, and everybody is at risk.

Our strange dilemma is that the human values we hold as individuals are routinely eviscerated by the inhuman systems we create to negate them in our consuming passion to distinguish and separate humans from other humans. We care about the poor, the disadvantaged, and the handicapped in the abstract, because there is always the abstract possibility that any of us as individuals could someday encounter poverty or disadvantage. But the fact that we create and defend with such vigor the very systems which produce and perpetuate poverty and disadvantage give a decidedly hollow ring to the care and concern we profess. The massive resistance to affirmative action reveals much about the confused state of American values. Some of the cases argued before the Supreme Court—*Bakke, Weber,* and *Fullilove,* for example—illustrate the ease and the cynicism with which the prior issues of human rights and simple justice can get lost in the tortuous labyrinth of specious counterclaims which would effectively nullify even that *minimum* gesture of moral concern that affirmative action is supposed to represent.

Affirmative action was conceived as a remedial approach to accumulated injustice and its long and tragic train of consequences. It is the official, belated recognition that America has a problem. It is not a *black* problem, and the problem with the Problem is that we have approached it so tardily, so tentatively, so testily, and without grace or moral conviction. The issue for us is not *who* locked African Americans out of competitive enterprise in America. We all know who. The real issue is who perpetuates the lockout from the all but impregnable bastions of accumulated racial privilege, and what will be done to loosen the coils of constriction a little bit. America's power, prestige, and national sense of purpose have been put to the test by two world wars in this century, and there has been a pervasive erosion of confidence in American leadership, and perhaps in the American Dream itself. Our national purpose is fragmented and confused, and the ominous symptoms of our cultural malaise are increasingly apparent. We seem incapable of learning from the past or planning effectively for the future. It was not very long ago that racism expressed in differential housing, black unemployment, segregation in education, and in most other practical aspects of our common existence caused our cities to be laid waste and our schools to become battlegrounds. But in spite of the hard lessons of the sixties, we still managed to profess surprise and shock when the seventies threatened a repeat of history—even though the breadlines in the black ghettos were longer than ever before, even though the Ku Klux Klan was resurgent all over the country, and even though the North had managed to outdo the South in devising ever new stratagems for maintaining de facto segregation in the public schools.

What is new in racial justice in America is so often what is old: a sombre tale that has been too long in the telling; a weary variation on a theme that never seems to find retirement. We cannot avoid the conclusion that few of the changes we hoped for have been truly accomplished, even though the cosmetics of progress are always being paraded before us with cynical reassurance. But believing comes hard, because the most convincing data are read not from the charts and the graphs, but in the baleful faces of the hopeless legions of the battered, the jobless, and the dispossessed who people the mean streets of this affluent nation.

In spite of our persistence in rejecting our own ideals, God has been gracious (or at least patient), and our country has become a mighty power in the world. America counts her bathtubs and television sets in the millions; despite the implosion of communism and the thawing of the cold war, our war machine is sufficiently intact to deter any aggressor, real or imagined. We have sent men to the moon and robots to the stars, and the Coca-Cola sign and the golden arches of McDonald's beckon the world for lighthearted refreshment in the most remote hamlets of this terrestrial globe. But there are people in Chicago and Atlanta and Washington, D.C., who are dying for want of bread. And there are people in Los Angeles and New York and Memphis whose principal struggle is to retain a last clutch on dignity before some impersonal behemoth of power and progress claims them for its provender.

The same fetters that bind the captive bind the captor, and the American people are captives to their own myths woven so cleverly into the fabric of our national experience. When our selective ignorance about what we do not want to know emerges as presumptive innocence *because* we didn't know, the casuistry designed to relieve us from responsibility has come full circle. We are the best-informed people on earth about everything except the virulence of race and place. President Ronald Reagan admitted to the American people with all the candor he could muster that before he was president he didn't even know that America *had* a race problem. Such a blatant rhetoric of innocence by reason of ignorance on the part of the leader of the world's foremost democracy must be disconcerting, to say the least, to the millions of the world's suppressed peoples who look to America as the symbol of the freedom they struggle for. The world is an amazing diversity of peoples we need to *know* about to care about. And if Americans prefer not to know in order to avoid the onus of caring, the world will turn elsewhere in search of more promising allies of freedom and liberation. Charity begins at home, and if we ever get through the mist and the murk of our self-willed naïveté, we will discover that our own social values have long since been corroded, the democratic ideal has been corrupted, and we have allowed ourselves to be transported by specious imaginings to a self-willed Shangri-la we know does not exist. Our most vivid imaginings are, alas! anchored in the dust of reality, and when the fantasy is spent it must come to rest in the very dust from which it took its flight.

President Reagan's sheltered innocence and Newt Gingrich's sarcastic solution-by-success formula notwithstanding, America does have a race problem. Unfortunate. Unnecessary. But true. And most Americans do know about it. But knowing about the problem is not quite the same as assessing it, addressing it, and eliminating it. The great majority of those who are willing to recognize the existence of a problem also recognize it as a "Negro problem" or a "black problem." It is not *their* problem, they reason; it is not even an American problem. It is, by conventional consensus, an *African American* problem, essentially caused by the simple *presence* of people of African descent in a "white man's country," and it will be completely resolved only when the Africans are no longer here. In the meantime, they say, Blacks ought to be held responsible for their disgusting plight, though there is little confidence that they have the will or the ability to address their deficits because they are inherent. Instead Blacks cry "victimization" in the effort to place the onus of their degradation on the shoulders of a generation of whites who were not even born when the black travail began. There is no limit to the cynicism that willful ignorance can produce.

In the conventional American mind, "crime" figures most prominently among the African American's social disabilities, with violence alleged to be the principal expression of an innate criminality. Whether or not there is validity in such a notion, these perceptions are deeply rooted in the psychology of the slave society which created "the nigger" in the first place and clothed him with a persona reflective of the society's principal fears and interests. The remarkable dictum that Africans were perpetual children requiring the white man's God-ordained oversight to restrain them from murder and rapine was an important cornerstone of the justification for their enslavement. Such notions die hard. Although the institution such ideas were designed to protect and rationalize had run its miserable course 150 years ago, the felt need for continuous justification of that historic misadventure, and the compelling convenience of a built-in, readily identifiable "It," or scapegoat, for every imaginable dissonance of human caprice has proven too great a political expedience, and too comforting a psychological palliative to sacrifice to social and moral reconstruction. For our moral recalcitrance, we Americans have paid and are paying an unconscionable forfeit in peace, justice, and understanding, not to mention the astronomical political and economic costs required to underwrite our willful addiction to racial chauvinism. All of the humanizing values of community have been lost, resulting in ersatz relational structures, and we are forever fumbling for some elusive gossamer of "truth" about ourselves and about each other to justify our self-determined alienation from each other. In the meantime, our problems of misperception beget massive problems of substance, which are compounded by our fear of beginning at the beginning in search of resolution.

It is easy to confuse violence with power because the two are so often packaged together, but they are not the same. Violence is the wanton, irresponsible *expression* of power. But power also comes in other guises: a word of comfort, a counsel of understanding, a signal of forgiveness, an evidence of caring, a declaration of solidarity—these are the exhibitions of power which need no violence to be effective.

THE BELEAGUERED BLACK MALE

Today the national focus is on the wanton elimination of the African American male from meaningful participation in the common ventures of American life. It is not just that young black males are being targeted by a weird convergence of hostile interests within and outside the black community. It is the black male *presence,* the black male, *period,* that America has declared expendable. The young black male gladiators are there, all right, preening and posturing and dying in their wretchedness before a full gallery of the morbidly unconcerned who have gathered to watch the mayhem from safe houses of noninvolvement. These are the young black males the media label "an endangered species." This time the media are right, but there may be an endangered ethic at stake as well. Perhaps it can be rejuvenated in time to save this most recent endangered species along with the snail darter, the four-eye crocus, the black-footed ferret, the gray wolf, and other such creatures pushed to the edge of extinction. But to date, the "endangered black male" seems to have stirred little national concern beyond containment and isolation.

The calculus of social determination describing the crisis of African American males is not all that complex. As a matter of fact, the factors that fuel the phenomenon are really quite elementary. Put simply and put bluntly, we are losing a vital asset indispensable to our survival as a culture *and* as a nation. We are losing men: *black men.* We are losing young black males in just about every way it is possible to forfeit human life and promise. There is a massive erosion of the successor generation of black males, who are so maimed by the circumstances of survival as to forfeit their anticipated potential as assets to the future of the black estate and the nation. Some of the sources of the problem, such as unemployment, undereducation, and miseducation, are obvious. Less obvious and more deadly are the hidden causes institutionalized in the normative patterns of American perception and behavior which in turn educe patterns of response among young blacks that yield a continuing fallout of alienation, criminalization, self-immolation, and incarceration.

Alienation means that a substantial segment of our next generation is estranged from most of the values we hold to be critical to the way we see ourselves, and to the way we think our lives should be lived, our interests should be defined, and our goals should be pursued. We have presumed these values to be self-evident, their inculcation to be osmotic, and their rewards to be consistent with the investment in their pursuit. And we have been wrong on all counts. The discovery that our conventional values are often fuzzy and confused, and that there is great inconsistency in the way they are sanctioned is a primary cause of the alienation of our youth; and the more painful the discovery experience, the more protracted the alienation is likely to become. Alienation is not just rebelliousness, it is the stage for a fundamental difference in worldview—that is, the way reality is perceived and interpreted. When alienation becomes "fixed," those alienated develop alternative values and alternative means for their realization. It is at this point that a counterculture emerges, and the gap between "us" and "them" widens into an abyss.

Alienation from the common values of society, the prevailing customs, and the approved way of looking at life and pursuing its interests sets the stage for *criminalization*. Approval demands conformity to the norms set by the controlling powers that be: political, religious, economic, social, whatever. Sometimes these controlling powers interlock in such a way as to make it virtually impossible for certain classes of citizens to survive within the constraints of the "approved" pursuit of interests that may be considered critical to life, welfare, and self-validation. When this happens, all those who are forced into alternative means of realizing the same goals common to the rest of society will be criminalized; that is, they will be forced into "unapproved" behaviors—*behavior outside the law*—and they will be branded and stigmatized accordingly. Recent statistics suggest that fully one quarter of all black males will bear the stigma of criminalization before they reach thirty, and once that stigma is affixed, it is difficult indeed for it to be forgiven or removed. Often the slate is never truly clean again, and the past stays on to haunt the future as long as there is a future to be haunted.

In due course, the ever-present threat of black criminalization produces self-immolation or black autopredation (i.e., preying on each other). *Black on Black*. In a society where the highest premium for approved behavior is refracted through a racial prism, inevitably criminalization takes on a racial cast. This means that whatever the circumstances, the highest percentage of those to be criminalized in America will be black; and it also means that there is a penalty differential between what must be paid for disapproved behavior against whites and what is paid for disapproved behavior against blacks. And since young black males are already considered presumptive candidates for criminalization, the penalty for disapproved or criminal behavior against blacks is the least certain and the least severe of all. This means that black on black crime enjoys a relative degree of immunity before the law and in the hierarchy of social disapproval. This in turn encourages black youth committed to alternative or extra-legal means of pursuing self-interest to believe that they will find it infinitely less hazardous to maim and kill each other for pittances, or for cathartic relief, than to risk the full weight of social disapproval and legal sanction that is certain to follow criminal behavior toward whites. The high incidence of destruction of Blacks by Blacks reflects the low esteem in which black youth (taking their cues from society) hold themselves and each other. Such low self-esteem may well be a factor in the apparent remorselessness, perhaps even eagerness, with which they kill each other, thereby wiping out the (valueless?) mirror images of themselves. They know that they are invisible people with nowhere to go and no way to get there. And if you are bound for nowhere in particular, is it not more exciting (*and cool?*) to get there with a bang than with a whimper? To be "cool" in the face of death may well be the only expression of dignity available in a lifetime.

Black life has always been cheap. *Too cheap.* But the going rate has been drastically undercut in recent times, and the prevailing threat to individual black existence no longer comes in dunce caps and bedsheets or in the official blue uniforms that once signaled the oppressive presence of "the law" in the concentration pens we euphoniously call the "inner city." Today death originates more often than not in the apartment next door, on the sidewalks out front, in the crack house down the block, or from the anonymous "hit wagon" cruising the neighborhood or patrolling the "turf." It is casual. It is impersonal. It is a way *out* of life. It requires no reason, no rationale; just the means and the opportunity. *Bang! Bang! You're dead. But you were born dead! And so was I.*

Incarceration is the final act of the criminalization process, and the most scarring. The United States has a million people behind bars, more per capita than any other country in the world. We may find a temporary relief from our sense of grossness in reasoning that only some of those people in cages are black. But that relief vanishes, and it ought to turn to horror, when we read on to learn that for each white person in jail in the United States, eight African Americans are there to keep him an awkward kind of company. We jail black men at the unconscionable rate of 3,109 for each 100,000 we permit to roam free. In pre-Mandellan South Africa, which imprisoned more people than any country except the United States, and where blacks outnumber whites five to one, the figures are almost benign by comparison: 730 black males in jail for every 100,000 blacks in the general population. It requires only a little simple arithmetic to discover that black people in what was once commonly held to be the most racially oppressive regime on earth were ten times *less* likely to have their freedom taken away from them than black citizens of the United States of America.

Obviously something has gone awry. There are racial gremlins inhibiting the proper access to the American Dream and the democratic process on which we have staked our freedom and tranquillity. The young black males in crisis are the immediate losers, but theirs is not the sum of the tragedy.

THE DESTRUCTIVENESS OF SELF-INTEREST

The alternative to an organized society, reasoned Thomas Hobbes, is a "state of nature," a dismal and unrewarding existence characterized by unlimited aggression and counteraggression; an existence in which every individual is a law unto himself, in which there is no definition of morality, and in which force and fraud are the respected instruments for the realization of self-interest, which, in the state of nature, is the sole factor of human motivation. Hobbes may or may not have provided an adequate explanation of what is happening in our society, but we must at least recognize that *any* society in which large numbers of people find life to be "solitary, nasty, mean, brutish, and short" is in trouble by whatever name. When the power which belongs to all the people is fraudulently and consistently manipulated for the preservation of selective interests, what stake have the disinherited and the oppressed in the maintenance of that society? To have the responsibilities of citizens and the disabilities of aliens is not a persuasive argument for law and order. In short, the game may not appear to be worth the candle.

Whenever the life chances of some are consistently manipulated by others, freedom is in contest and dignity is in peril. Where freedom and dignity have been seriously compromised, people who may not know what they are precisely, are nevertheless sensitive to the absence of something vital, an absence which deadens their lives and eliminates their meaningful participation in the significant experiences of the human enterprise. Freedom implies power—the power to be responsible. Freedom without power is mockery; life without dignity is simply absurd.

Today, there are deep suspicions that the power which defines America is at best morally indifferent, and that America as a society has come perilously close to abandoning the notion that justice is possible, or even desirable, and that morality is a factor of consequence in either social relations or individual well-being. Our prime commitment seems to be to expedience, and since neither justice nor morality lends itself to mere opportunism, what is "right" seems increasingly to be equated with whatever bobs up with persistence in the ebb and flow of human intercourse. Justice, like the price of pork bellies, becomes a function of the market, and morality is reduced to whatever it takes to keep the market active.

Our distorted sense of justice at home often sends us rushing off to settle the world's problems in the style which we still imagine best exemplifies our national image. But the national image we cherish so much at home and want so desperately to export to the world is at serious odds with the way we are often perceived abroad. To much of the world we are still "the ugly Americans."

The enormous toll we are required to pay for the privilege of being hated is diffused in the mist of our national egomania as we rush hither and thither (noblesse oblige!) in our efforts to export our American principles and values to remote corners of the globe, despite the fact that our own camp is in serious disarray. Here at home, too often the professional brokers to whom we entrust our moral investments are not themselves the best evidence of serious commitment. In consequence, the moral leadership of our seminal institutions is frequently quite shallow and unconvincing. Government, religion, communications, education, and even the family are all susceptible and suspect. Moral management by consignment or by consensus is restructuring our moral patterning through the casual, almost subliminal substitution of so-called alternative values designed to erase the age-old distinctions between up and down, right and wrong, the beautiful and the monstrous.

Today, we are invited to believe that the only real responsibility people have is to themselves and their own gratification, and that all moral alternatives are equally valid since they have no meaningful reference beyond the self. Cloaked in the casuistry of our "new" sophistication, this ancient, convenient nonsense is no less destructive for all its cleverness. And it is no less vulgar for all the notables who endorse it when they prostitute themselves to the cheap opportunism the retreat from responsibility always signifies. But it *is* confusing, for we live in a time when the issues of social intercourse are exceedingly complex, and the parameters of personal and social responsibility grow more indistinct with each new problem we are called upon to confront. In recent times the enduring problem of racism has been joined by such formidable issues as abortion, euthanasia, bioengineering, nuclear energy, technocracy, and the abuse of the environment. Ironically, these are all of a piece. They are all new expressions of our troubled understanding about the value of human life and the inalienable rights which accrue to it.

CIVILIZED DECADENCE

The price of freedom is the risk that it may be corrupted or taken away by perverse ideologies which claim shelter under its umbrella, and the decline of great civilizations is characteristically initiated by internal assaults on their systems of value. If the eternal verities by which society is ordered can be forced into question, if the good, the true, and the beautiful can be challenged openly and without fear, that is democracy. But if that which is patently and inherently evil and degrading can be successfully masqueraded as a reasonable "alternative" to that which affirms human life, human dignity, and human responsibility, then we need not worry about armies of invasion. The civilization where this can happen is self-committed to dissolution and demise.

We have never come close to realizing the "righteous empire" which excited the Puritan founders of this society, but we seem farther from the ideal now than ever before. Our minds are keener, our perceptions are more acute, our information is more prodigious, but our selfish inconsistency disarms our determination to succeed. Somehow we have managed to survive a half century of domestic tension and turmoil. The Feverish Fifties, the Savage Sixties, the Sensual Seventies, and the Excessive Eighties are mercifully behind us, but their harvest is still to be winnowed. The "strange fruit" that once hung from the magnolias with regularity is no longer a celebration of our decadence. The schoolhouse door has lost its attraction for political posturing. The cattle prods are sheathed; the snarling attack dogs have been leashed; the church bombers have cached most of their dynamite; and the storm troopers have come out from behind their dark glasses and scraped the gore from their billy clubs. Surfeited with blood, and reproved by the world for our savagery, we persist in fitfully trying to blot out the reality of the past that haunts us. But reality will not go away, and to recognize reality is to return to responsibility. We cannot undo the past. The errors our fathers made are interred with them. The errors we make begin with us, and they sprout at *our* feet, not at the feet of our fathers. We cannot erase the past, but we can learn from it in the interest of a new kind of future.

CLEANSING THE NATIONAL CONSCIENCE

We still have to learn that there is evil in the world, and that to compromise with evil in any of its guises is to be destroyed by it. When the beast walks among us, we will either restrain it, or it will hold us captive in our own houses. A system of values without consistency is patently incapable of ordering a society so complex as our own. Perhaps this is what Russian critic Solzhenitsyn meant when he said that it is Americans' devotion to the letter of the law rather than its intention that paralyzes the country's ability to defend itself against the corrosion of evil.

The whole history of America has been the odyssey of a confident society in search of its potential as a truly great civilization to become the justification of its own self-perception. If that effort has at times been somewhat less than heroic, there have been enough moments of great promise to keep the dream alive. The soul we pledged in return for the dubious tinsel of being "master" to a captive people is still in escrow. Slavery is the deliberate abuse of power and privilege in the arbitrary reduction of other humans to a lesser category of being, and it compromises selected human possibility in an invidious personal interest which negates the divine prerogatives by which human beings are defined. Only murder, which is the arbitrary summary termination of the whole spectrum of human possibility, is more conclusive in its negation. Hence, to live with the record of the centuries is to confront daily the fallen ethics of a civilization we hold to be ordained by God for loftier possibilities.

But slavery is revocable; and America did in fact make that revocation almost 150 years ago. What we failed to do, however, was revoke the ideology and repudiate the conventions that made slavery an anomalous institution in a Christian society self-consciously dedicated to freedom. But *racism in America is not the lingering memorabilia of slavery.* That is a misconception, the recognition of which uncovers new and unplumbed possibilities for its eradication. The truth is that slavery was merely the political institutionalization of a preexisting ideology. It was an *existing* racism that redefined Indians and Africans alike for the ambitious economic and social convenience of Europeans bent on the maximization of a new world of opportunities they were unprepared to confront with their own labor. It is of critical importance to have at last a clear understanding of the order of circumstances which still hold us hostage to a past that is beyond reconstruction. Because we have mistakenly assumed American racism to be a sort of normative and necessary aftermath of slavery, we have tended to believe that with time it will recede from our consciousness and wither from our institutions. It is time now to recognize that we have rested our hopes for deliverance upon the wrong set of presuppositions.

The recognition that racism anteceded slavery, and not the other way around, calls for a more active remedy than the placebo of "time" affords. To our credit, we did eventually revoke that "peculiar institution," but there we stopped, waiting for time to do the rest. What we in fact revoked was a practice rather than the ideology which created the practice, justified its existence, and corrupted all of our cardinal systems of value. But since we dismantled the *institution*, and that begrudgingly, we have done little to cleanse the national conscience of the virulence which still festers there 150 years after the structure of slavery was repudiated. We remain a tortured nation because we have confused the elimination of the most prominent symptoms of our distress with a cure which has yet to be accomplished.

Our national malaise is a pervasive, debilitating "melancholia," to borrow a term from the slave era, and that melancholia derives from an acute sense of moral wretchedness over the silent recognition of an ethic that failed in a historic surrender to expediency and avarice. But our many protestations of personal innocence from the entails of our national history bring us no relief because we have not clearly distinguished the fact of history from the sense of obligation to justify it *after the fact*. We can do nothing about the reality of an act that is past; history cannot be recalled, despite the astrology of contemporary revisionism. What *was* remains in fact what it was. But we can and we must separate ourselves from the psychological trauma of a history we did not commit, *and which does not require our endorsement* for its justification. The justifications for the dehumanization and enslavement of the Africans were invented *before* the fact. They were institutionalized *in* the fact, and they died *with* the fact. Let them rest where they are. They belong to another time, another order, another civilization. They do not belong to us, or to our children. We are beyond the past. It is irrevocable, and our chief loyalties must be to the future, to a new beginning.

VII

INTO THE MULTICULTURE

America . . .

The ancient ways

The laws I kept

The Gods I knew

Are gone

How can I know those ways again?

What am I if I am not

American?

—C. ERIC LINCOLN,

This Road since Freedom

The iceman cometh, but the fire is already here. As we prepare for the transition from a relatively pedestrian black-and-white society to the formidably complex true multiculture spilling over the horizon, we would do well to anticipate the more likely sources of the problems that lie ahead and assess our available resources for dealing with them. As we probe more intensively the shifting parameters of the developing multiculture which is already re-shaping life and living here in the United States, too little is being asked, too little is being said, and practically nothing of conse-quence is being done to ease our transit from the harsh, inflexible conventions of yesterday toward the gentler, more humane and caring society tomorrow will demand as the minimum investment in our national survival.

Our very first responsibility is the sober recognition that the approaching challenges are not mere escalations of those we left behind without truly solving them in the decades of domestic turmoil we have managed to weather thus far. Some of those old, unsolved problems will surely resurface to bedevil us in new and unfamiliar configurations, but they will hardly constitute the sum of the agenda of multiculturalism. That agenda may well include most of the particularities of expectation expressed in the benign dreams of Martin Luther King, but it will be a vastly different order of expectation deriving from a more multifarious spectrum of values presented in unaccustomed settings of urgency. For 350 years or so, our most critical social problem revolved around de-fining and establishing a place and a space for the "niggers" we had created, and keeping them in it with such minimum modifi-cations as evolving exigencies might urge upon us from time to time. That age has ended. It was over in prospect even before the silent specter of multiculturalism began looking over the national shoulder to try to discern the national intent. Were we still in the business of nigger making, or had we reached a maturity in which the diverse peoples of the world could find the respect and freedom we bragged about abroad? From a distance the signals were mixed, but the political and economic urgencies for most prospective new Americans were compelling and unrelenting. So they came on faith—faith in the dream they had heard about for so long, but unsure of whether that dream was palpable.

These new Americans of the multiculture come from the four corners of the earth, but for the most part they are the consequences of our foreign adventures come home to us—people whose lives we have disrupted, whose national integrity we have impugned, whose cultures we have degraded, whose politics we have corrupted, whose resources we have coveted, commandeered, taken away, or raffled off in our capacity as power broker for the world. They are proud peoples; many are of ancient lineage, and all are entitled to the full complement of respectful appreciation and dignity reserved for the human species. They should not have to demand it; it is the inalienable common property of the human endowment. But they *will* demand it—and more—if it is denied them. Unlike the old-line African minority, these new Americans, although many have known and lived with the inconveniences of political oppression, have not been so recently traumatized by the dehumanization of abject slavery. Their perspectives on the meaning of color and culture will seldom be in consonance with conventional American perspectives on the critical issues of race and place. Most of these new Americans have not come to serve some would-be surrogates of the divine presence; they have come to cast their common lot with the Americans who "discovered" them, "rescued" them, and beguiled them with the wonders of Christian democracy back home in the land of the free, the home of the brave and the just. Now they have come to see for themselves, to be a part of that ideal civilization: *To be Americans!* But it will not be all Disneyland and apple pie. Can we meet the challenges implicit in the new sharing we will be called upon to entertain? The ball is in the home court. America, take notice.

There are no legitimate degrees of citizenship in America. Either one is a citizen "with all the rights, privileges and responsibilities thereunto appertaining," or one is not a citizen at all. The quasi citizenship that characterized the black estate for so many generations will not work in the multiculture that is here and coming. We cannot niggerize half the peoples of the world. God forbid that we should try. But even as the potential new Americans gather from the exotic cultures of the world and settle in to test the fabled waters of a free and democratic society, the old-stock African American retainees are still playing out scenarios by T. S. Eliot and W. H. Auden:

> We are the hollow men
> We are the stuffed men
> Leaning together
> Headpiece filled with straw.
> —T. S. Eliot, "The Hollow Men"

> Shall we never be asked for? Are we simply
> Not wanted at all?
> —W. H. Auden, *The Age of Anxiety*

THE TRAUMA OF TRANSITION

We can do a lot to ease the transition from a black-and-white polarity to a viable multicultural society if we begin with the self-cleansing recognition that we are captives of a past we did not invent. If we have no responsibility for the errors in judgment of past generations, then, mutatis mutandis, we have no responsibility for perpetuating a defensive ideology which proves nothing beyond our stamina for perversity. We know in our more reverential moments that we cannot turn the clock back to where it was, but we shrink from disengagement because we have confused a mere ideological expedience with loyalty to a way of life that, if it ever was, can never be again. Racism holds the racist captive with his victim. Neither is free to be the self of choice. As a result, for the individual caught up in the ideology of racism, to ever veer from the prescribed conventions is to run the risk of the most primitive sanctions. That is our Babylonian captivity—

the self-enforcement of the racial party line. But the party line loses a little credibility each day as reality catches up with "settled history." Ultimately, the myths we live by must answer to their contradictions. When faith falters, false gods tumble down.

There have always been color-blind individuals whose moral commitments transcend ideology in favor of people, and whose sense of ought does not find its fulfillment in the consensus of a discredited convention. The travail of alienation may be no less intense because of their intrepidness, of course, but these rugged outposts in the flood have on occasion slowed the momentum of social erosion long enough to stave off the consummate triumph of evil. There are such people, and America will need them as it moves forward into the future. They will pay for the privilege of their convictions, but the cost will be small when compared with the price of saying nothing and doing less.

CRACKS IN THE COLOR CURTAIN

In recent times there has been a very tentative willingness to moderate the language of racist ideology somewhat to avoid the obsolescence of the extremes implied in "black" or "white." The term biracial (borrowed from another lexicon) is heard now and then. Biracial denies in effect the age-old allegation that "one drop of 'Negro' blood makes one a 'Negro' with all of his or her succeeding generations." The new usage would seem to imply the genetic parity of the parents but apparently still presumes them to be racially "pure" or discrete. This, I take it, is progress—of a sort. It was never very clear to me how black people could be considered "inferior" when they were so genetically potent that a single black gene could completely neutralize centuries of white "blue blood" and make a "Negro" out of the finest genealogy all those generations of Aryan ancestry could produce. Ironically, the Black Muslims of Elijah Muhammad's day resolved the mystery and converted it to their own offensive by pursuing to its logical conclusion a doctrine that had been the substance of law and convention in America for three hundred years. The superpotency of black blood was quite real, Elijah argued. In fact it was so real that it represented the difference between good and evil, between black men and blue-eyed devils, a conclusion quite in reverse of that intended by conventional racism. Black was "true color," the Muslims decided, and white, no color at all. Hence dominant black would overwhelm white whenever the two were in contact, with predictable results in any logical evaluation of racial patterning. But Elijah Muhammad—with a fourth-grade education—was ridiculed for his "grotesque genetic theories," even though he borrowed them wholesale from the prevailing precepts of American law and custom. The ideology of racism sometimes makes for strange bedfellows.

TRANSRACIAL ADOPTIONS

Of far greater significance today is the still tentative trend toward transracial adoptions. The critical motivations for such adoptions are, of course, wide ranging, and some will have little if any significance for breaches in the racist ideology underpinning our system of social relations. For example, the supply of white children for adoption has been quite low for many years, and Americans who wanted children often managed to acquire them (at great expense) in Europe or elsewhere. While African American children in need of parents have always been in plentiful supply, there was practically no demand for them until quite recently, partly because bureaucracy and convention were solidly against cross-racial or cross-religious adoptions, and partially because it was a taboo which could bring down icy ridicule and other reprisals on any who dared experiment with it. Not infrequently, some African Americans added their objections to the more massive white antipathy.

It is high time to rethink the issues involved. Tens of thousands of Colonel Bascombe's children have been parented by Blacks without apparent injury; and if the Colonel's "legitimate" kin now want to return the courtesy in the common social interest, it is a gesture of timely significance and not one to be derailed by the conventions of yesterday. Whatever the impetus of motivation, the lives and welfare of children are at stake in a society that *must* change and is changing. The African American child of this generation is in extraordinary peril, and all other judgments must address that reality, in the interest of the child, despite the reasons for the trauma that grips the majority of black families. The extended family that was once the critical edge of black survival has long since succumbed to the exigencies of the sky-rise ghettos and the interlocking contrivances of social dependency. African Americans without jobs are incapable of supporting their own children, and African Americans with jobs either do not feel secure enough to risk taking on another uncertain responsibility, or the bitter memories of having to raise and love the Colonel's cuckoldry in their own homes for so many centuries has made them wary. The laws of the slave era protected the Colonel (and his entail) from the consequences of his lust by declaring: "The father of a slave is unknown." Or, to put it more delicately: every slave is by definition *nullius filius,* literally, a "son of nobody." So the sons and daughters of nobody became the children of the black family by default—in and out of slavery. Slavery as an institution has long since screeched and bumped and rattled its way into history, but not into oblivion, for some of its legacies live on to exacerbate the enduring struggle to be done with it once and for all. Although the outrage of *nullius filius* as law collapsed with that "peculiar institution," its ideology still haunts us, and the Colonel has shown no convincing interest in retiring from his gallantry. Black stances on adoption will moderate as the fledgling black middle class feels more confirmed in its status and in its contingent social responsibilities and expectations. But that is a future that is not yet, and until it arrives the disastrous plight of African American children will not be substantially relieved by African American adoption.

While the salvage of innocent lives is the principal argument for transracial adoption, it is by no means the only one. Since racism begins in the home and finds its reinforcements in outside associations, there is potential advantage in being able to start undoing the racial mischief at its source. There the opportunity is immediate and palpable, twenty-four hours a day. True, there may also be some psychological risk for the child in question, but that is a speculation that must be measured against the probability of a more consummate trauma had the adoption not occurred. The options available in this life are seldom ideal, but they presuppose a moral power beyond human choice to redress the balance and even up the odds. In a society where we must surely be anticipating new ventures in social relations as a multi-culture, transracial marriage is already firmly established in law and increasingly common in practice. Hence, we ask a rhetorical question: If transracial marriage is here, and biracial children are here, can transracial adoptions be far behind? Actually, "racial" disparity between many parents and children has long been en-demic to the culture though tacitly ignored. Transracial adoption would seem to give social recognition to the fact that love and concern for each other are functions of our humanity and not limited by race and place. Many who would agree have legitimate reservations about the risks of humanitarianism falling princi-pally on the backs of our children, but our children are already at the most extreme risk possible, just for being alive and black. Can responsible transracial adoption be so much worse?

CHANGE AND POWER

Change today is the best assurance of social health and public order for tomorrow. America is changing, of course, but whether the rate and the direction argue for better or for worse is a ques-tion we have not addressed with sufficient energy or determina-tion. We are accustomed to measuring significant change in terms of how it affects our cornerstone conventions, which are anchored in racial goals or prerogatives we tend to equate with life itself. While this may be a very revealing commentary on the world's most advanced civilization here on the eve of the twenty-first cen-tury, the fundamental issue is *not* race but power. The true issue is *power* and how it is distributed and abused through the construc-tion and maintenance of a racial index of eligibility—a system of social regulations and management which is suddenly obso-lete. In the stark simplicity of a black-and-white society where there was no middle ground between polarities, such a strategy could work indefinitely because the repressive conditioning was focused on a single, allegedly unmistakable target. But it was a strategy for which the apostles of power paid an inordinate toll in moral condemnation, and possibly in self-respect and peace of mind as well. It was a strategy rife with religious and political incongruities, and one which frequently required the people who contrived it to deny their own words and principles, and most tragic of all, their own sons and daughters, with legal and conventional fictions of incredible temerity.

In a multicultural society, the convenient polar extremes of black *or* white pay diminishing returns in efficiency for determining who is to be excluded from the circle of power and privilege. The visual racial index is no longer convincing (it never was foolproof), and the assault on the legal infrastructure protecting the system which began with *Brown* vs. *Board of Education* forty years ago has continued to whittle away at the foundations. Other "racial" and nonracial minorities suing for the right to be human have broadened the assault and accelerated it, and the once-vaunted color differential between people who are black and people who are white is crowded with newcomers who are neither. How, then, shall we make our decisions in the future on who is eligible to share power and responsibility and who is not, if the racial signposts are too blurred to read with the precision we used to know, or thought we knew. We could try apartheid, of course, and simply declare by fiat who is what without total dependence on the shifting sands of color. But alas! The ink is not quite dry on the last judgment on that unholy conspiracy:

> The seed was sown
> the weed was grown
> the burr was blown
> the weed was gone.
> —C. Eric Lincoln, unpublished poem

The lessons from South Africa are that people are no less people because they are not mirror images of each other, and that race and place can never effectively be matched with each other because the premise behind the theory is fraudulent to begin with. *Race is a fantasy.* A chimera. A stalking-horse for power and privilege. Most Americans know that, of course, because the protective façade of selective ignorance has long since been demolished. But to know the truth is not necessarily to act on it, and the captivity of race and place remains the problem of the twentieth century, and the threat to the twenty-first. Nevertheless, the tide of the times does not favor an indefinite tenure for such socially destructive anachronisms, and the most tractable candidate for yesterday's managed exploitation may well be the leader of tomorrow's most determined resistance. The "wretched of the earth," and most particularly the battered peoples of the world who survived the awesome carnage of World War II, have developed some new notions about themselves and what lies behind their wretchedness. Their survival amongst the debris of the vaunted structures of power that lay toppled about them suggested that the fixed destiny they had accepted for generations was not so fixed after all. It pays to look closely at whatever masquerades as the hand of God; there may be a wart of avarice between the fingers. In any case there was a new awakening among the world's conventional niggers which suggested to them that the abuse they suffered was unnatural, unwarranted, unremitting, and unnecessary. It is now clear that it was also unacceptable, as the escalating brushfires of civil unrest all over the world register the people's impatience with the way things used to be. The sword of Damocles hangs uncertainly over the heads of the conventional masters of self-designated privilege as the people who have been shut out clamor for redress outside the courtyards of their exclusion. It has nothing whatever to do with race. It is humanity struggling to reclaim itself, to be recognized, to be what it is capable of becoming. It is not a matter of race; it is a matter of power. It is not an issue of place; it is an issue of privilege. If there is no disjunction between race and place and power and privilege in the society we have constructed for ourselves, it is time to change it for our children. Surely they deserve better than what they seem likely to receive.

BLACK RACISM?

In America racism is usually understood to mean *white* racism; that is, pejorative or prejudicial attitudes and behaviors attributed to white people with reference to Blacks or others who are not white; but occasionally allegations of black racism are also heard. Such allegations present an interesting paradox deriving from the assumption that racism is limited to attitude and ideology, when in fact its most traumatic expression is in behavior. Racism depends on power—the power of social consensus by which a self-designated quorum of individuals conspire together to secure to themselves exclusive, or near exclusive, control over scarce values or limited resources. At stake are such common desirables as wealth, respect, education, dignity, fame, creature comforts, and whatever else the society associates with consummate satisfaction, or that creates a posture of distinctiveness and privilege for its possessors.

"Race" is the arbiter determining membership or exclusion, and "color" is the principal index by which race is determined in the absence of exhaustive genetic validation. In consequence, any given population desiring to practice "racism" could in theory do so if it had the power of consensus that comes from mutual recognition of who is within and who is beyond the pale. Membership is by birthright confirmed by consensus. Consensus is also the coercive force which monitors and controls the behavior of the group with respect to designated others. There are no solitary racists. Racism is a group phenomenon, the practice of which requires a substantial, consistent, reliable lode of like-minded sentiment constantly "on-line" for gate keeping and maintenance. The power of group consensus is the critical instrument of social control. When that group constitutes a very large majority vis-à-vis other groups competing for common values in the same society, the power potential is magnified by a ratio reflecting the finite numbers respectively engaged. But when large numbers of individuals within the exclusive consensus are independent sources of power controlling critical decisions in employment, education, media, government, and so on, the power potential of racism is suddenly astronomical.

African Americans are not immune from any of the pejorative sentiments which fuel racist ideology. As individuals, they, like their counterparts in other self-designated groupings, cover the entire spectrum of human plausibility. But the implementation of racist ideology requires sustained, dependable quantums of power—consensual and discrete. Without that power black racism will never be any more than a voice of defiant impotence screaming out its frustrations against the evil already in place. It is a notion with nowhere to go and no way to get there. That is as it should be. One kettle of putrifaction is enough. While new configurations of alliance and power are bound to develop as the new realities of multiculture address the more pathological patterns of relationships we have indulged in the past, there should be no mandate and no necessity for the replication of an institution which has already done so much to demean and impoverish us all. There are less traumatic ways to resolve our differences and find a common peace in a common security.

BLACK VICTIMIZATION?

Racism produces its own mystique, and since its ideological underpinnings rest on fantasy, it is inevitable that the protective mystique which surrounds it should run toward the fantastic. For example, the alleged moral and intellectual incapacity of black people was one of the earliest "justifications" for their isolation and abuse. The list of similar fantasies of convenience is limited only by the constraints of imagination. One of the more recent is the theory of "victimization," which alleges that black people welcome defamation and abuse because it excuses them from the need to struggle for their own survival and exempts them from all moral responsibility. Such nonsense would scarcely warrant the dignity of refutation except that like all mythology, if heard often enough it may find its self-fulfillment in the selective convenience of its hearers. The truth is that however tragic and unjust the experience of racial victimization may be, it offers no immunities from personal struggle, and no reprieves from moral responsibility. Victimization *can* be a chastening experience, and when it is so perceived it may well yield a serendipitous insight which broadens the understanding of human frailty and moderates the instinct for reprisal. This is learning from a very painful experience, but neither the pain nor the experience confers any exemptions from ordinary responsibility, or any rewards for the inconveniences of color. In consequence, men and women of whatever race, color, or circumstance have to work out their salvation with God, and their differences with each other.

Some "self-evident" racial myths are often beyond the reach of reason or the mandates of morality because the initial reality, whatever it may have been, has become so encrusted with the accumulated barnacles of hatred as to defy reconstruction or identification. In such a case a rabid racist evaluation becomes its own justification because the emotional investment in it is a critical part of the sensory set by which it is perceived. It is like saying "a nigger is a nigger is a nigger because he acts like the nigger that he is," which is tautological nonsense to everyone except the tortured individual whose own sense of self is projected through his racial hostility. If there were no "niggers" to be the "niggers" who people his stygian world of racially devalued humanity, the racist's sense of his own self worth would be greatly diminished. In the wrenching, convoluted trial of O. J. Simpson that ran for almost a year in Los Angeles in 1995, the country stood aghast at the wanton racial viciousness of American law enforcement as it was exposed by the swaggering confessions of Los Angeles police detective Mark Fuhrman. In a series of interviews taped by Laura McKinny, a N.C. screenwriter, Detective Fuhrman spoke for hours on end, detailing the *routine* falsification of evidence, destruction of evidence, deliberate false arrest, beating and torture of prisoners, and connivance of officers of the law in a code of silence designed to deprive black citizens—"niggers" as Mark Fuhrman insisted on calling them—of their minimum rights before the law.

If America was aghast, it was either because our sensors for the wretched evidence of racist viciousness have been turned off or because the circuits are overloaded. Certainly there were no African Americans "aghast" at Mark Fuhrman's revelations. African Americans know such behavior to be routine, not just in Los Angeles, but in Atlanta, Chicago, Philadelphia, Podunk, and wherever white men see law enforcement as a proper expression of white rule. A gallows joke making the rounds at the time of Fuhrman's exposure told of a black male who was arrested because he had a Band-Aid on his lip. "Prime evidence," the arresting officer testified, "that the suspect burned his lips trying to blow up a city bus." The judge gave him "thirty years for the oral abuse of the tail pipes of a public vehicle." When the judicial system shares the conventional law enforcement point of view, as is so often the case, it is not hard to imagine where these skewed statistics on black criminalization come from: *they originate at the point where the Fuhrmanization of law enforcement and the Fuhrmanization of justice come together in a synthesis of doom. Black doom.* This is true victimization. But there can be no psychology of victimization until there are "victims" to endorse it. And if such a psychology does in fact exist, the cure would seem to be at least as obvious as the cause.

BLACK VIOLENCE?

Perhaps the most pervasive syndrome characterizing contemporary America is fear. We are a people afraid, and our growing uneasiness is reflected in the billions we spend on chemical narcosis, our sexual mania, and the proliferating opportunities to opt out of reality. It is not the fear generated by the cold war. The Russians are not coming, at least not now, except to harvest the rewards we always manage to hold in reserve for people who suddenly decide they don't hate us anymore. Nor is it the fear of the proliferation of nuclear capability that might conceivably place the button of global destruction within the reach of some madman, presumably one madder than the rest of the members of the "nuclear club" who already have that capability. As a matter of fact, there are few threats from outside the United States that Americans appear to be genuinely concerned about.

But we do have an internal problem which threatens the foundations of the freedom we hold to be the hallmark of our civilization, and which ramifies in other concerns buried deep in the American psyche. Suddenly there is a consciousness that we are a nation at risk. *Internal risk.* It is not the first time in our two hundred years of national sovereignty that we have been a nation at risk, but it is the first time that the sense of personal peril has been so pervasive and so conspicuous in the structures and strategies we have been compelled to raise to contain it. And just what is it we are afraid of? *We are afraid of each other.* The specter of violence walks among us and holds us hostage to ourselves. This is a desperate commentary on the quality of life in the world's most advantaged society. *Where have all the flowers gone?* And why are we armed to the teeth by day, imprisoned in our homes by night, and constantly tuned in to the news we dread so much to hear? Where have all the flowers gone? Someone plucked them, every one! We have met the enemy, and he is us!

FICTIONAL VALUES

One of the reasons America is under siege by the violence we ourselves have created is our refusal to take seriously the values we profess as having consequential impact upon the quality of life this society can expect to deliver. A practicum of values about the meaning of life and the definition of humanity is the minimum distinction which separates a civilization from a mere state of nature. But if that schedule of values is fictional or counterfeit, that will eventually be discovered, and the social consensus built on it will sooner or later collapse into predictable chaos. There are some values which must be fundamental to every civilized society, and from these, other values may be seen as derivative. These fundamental values include life, dignity, creativity, and responsibility.

It is well to reflect on these elements of the human imprimatur when we try to sort out the roots and the ramifications of the violence which grips America. The conventional presumption is that violence in America is an intrinsic hallmark of the African American presence. While that notion is patently untenable for any who have bothered to read American history and development, it is a myth of remarkable tenacity, and one of vast psychological and economic convenience for those for whom selective illiteracy functions as an alternative morality. So deeply does the association of blacks with violence saturate the interstices of the uncritical mind that our whole system of jurisprudence is compromised by that presumption, and the possibilities of fair and simple justice before the law are always encumbered. Some African Americans are violent, of course. Some are not. But are African Americans *as a people* more inclined to violence as a means of conflict resolution or in the promotion of perceived interests than are other Americans? Very probably not, conventional statistics notwithstanding. The truth will probably never be known, because the truth is irretrievably enmeshed in the vicious circle of evidence derived from its own presumptions. In consequence, to accept the grotesquely inflated ratio of racial violence implied in our official reckoning is to ignore the evidence of history, which after all may be the only reliable index we have.

How we see ourselves and how we perceive each other have vast implications for how we behave, and may contribute significantly to the covert sources of violence and potential violence. For example, although African Americans constitute only about 10 percent of the population, the conventional presumption of black criminality influences the incarceration of an unconscionable eight African Americans for every white person behind bars—a ratio which suggests that Blacks and whites do not even share the same universe insofar as criminal behavior is concerned. The most tragic consequence of this fantasy is that incarceration under such circumstances carries with it a long train of attendant abuses and consequences. Criminalization drastically increases the barriers between those criminalized by our social lacunae and the rest of society, with the predictable assurance that there will be more, and more, and more to pay for our shortsightedness.

Americans like to imagine themselves affronted by the murder and mayhem which holds selective sections of our great cities hostage to a criminal element we ourselves created. But there is cynicism and hypocrisy implicit in our willingness to be shocked by such violence, for violence has always been an integral part of our way of life. It began with a determined effort to exterminate the Native American, and it was confirmed as the most practical modus vivendi in our protracted effort to dehumanize the African as a justification for his enslavement. This process of chattelization produced a vast catalog of violent behavior ranging from flogging and branding to rape and murder. It is hard to make the case that human life and its attendant values are characteristically sacred to Americans as a people in spite of our repeated commitments to the principals of the human imprimatur. The evidence to the contrary is vividly illustrated in our most popular scenarios, fixed on the video screens twenty-four hours a day, splashed across the front page of every edition of the press, enacted in the public streets, the schools, and even in our most private asylums every time the clock ticks.

We still need to learn that every life has value. *All* life has value, and that is the tragic wastefulness of violence. It is only when life has been terminated that all possibility for creative development comes to an end. The dead soldier will never sue for peace; the electrocuted prisoner will never prove his innocence; the aborted fetus will never have a chance to say "thank you for loving me"; the young black male shot down patrolling a turf he thought was his will never know how wrong he was, or why. There are no reprieves if you're dead.

Perhaps it is time to give God back his options and honestly forswear the wanton violence that is strangling human possibility before it has had a fair chance to flower. But we cannot do this if we permit ourselves to be narcotized by the statistics that locate the problem of violence among selected populations. Violence is everywhere in America. In a society where killing is as common as Coca-Cola, Blacks kill, whites kill, cops and robbers kill each other. Parents kill their children born and unborn; children kill their parents at home, their teachers at school, and their playmates wherever they happen to play. Where violence is so permissive and so acceptable, it can hardly be charged off as black criminality. It is a national phenomenon, and like the drug traffic, the decline of civility, the dissolution of the family, and the resurgence of racism in all of its hideous guises, it is dragging us all into the yawning vortex of social and political recidivism.

Finally, whether presumptive black violence is a chimera of consolation or merely the tip of the iceberg of a general recession in the human struggle to be better than we are, the situation cannot be remedied by our popular philosophies and strategies of containment by the isolation of its presumptive sources. In the first place, we had already determined a policy of racial isolation long before we decided that black violence was our reason for doing it. And second, violence is pervasive in the culture and its perpetrators come in all colors, and there is no effective way of isolating the whole culture from itself. Nevertheless, we persist in the effort to create artificial concentrations of violence in selective spaces where it is still hoped that it can either be controlled or ignored, if only to give credence to the chauvinisms we can't seem to shed.

Ironically, the poor, the black, and the faceless have never been free of the shadow and the experience of violence, whether under color of law or simply through the tacit consensus of responsible people for whom the law is selectively optional. The rivers and bayous of the rural South, like the streets and alleys of the black ghettos of urban America, have a long, sad tale to tell about violence, and about the forces which converge in the selection of its principal victims. Nevertheless, it is false comfort to rest on the presumptive statistics which make violence a phenomenon of the ghetto. Human sensitivity is deadened by the implied license for selective aggression, and whenever violence is permitted or urged upon an "approved" target, sooner or later the lines become blurred and one target becomes as acceptable as another. It is madness to believe that the forces we have loosed or permitted in this society against the black, the poor, and the disinherited will retain the power of discrimination. *A dog gone mad knows no master—only the taste of blood!*

Suddenly we are aware that the old strategies of accusation, isolation, and containment have broken down, and that the pavilions of privilege and the tenements of terror are one in the nostrils of the beast that walks among us. Now there is a clarion call for the quick fix: more jails, more cops, more penalties, and more guns along with more cynicism and more political posturing. In short, more effort to shore up the bankrupt conventional wisdom which brought us to our present predicament in the first place. But I hear no call for more food, more housing, more jobs, more health care, and more opportunities to enable the ordinary people to live with the dignity and the sense of responsibility that make violence a less attractive way of life.

Where have all the flowers gone?

There is something happening in America which, in our moments of reflection, leaves us all with a pervasive feeling of uneasiness. Perhaps "all" is too inclusive, because there are increasing numbers of us who, by design and intention, have no moments of reflection, and want none. That leaves the rest of us who care about each other and who care about America to take up the ever-increasing slack from those who care only about themselves and their frantic moment in the sunlight of personal gratification. If America is in travail, and it is, then Whites and Blacks, Blacks and Whites, and all others who care must call upon themselves and upon each other to stand firm for what is right as the angry waters of pent-up rage and resentment rush over the sham-works of bigotry and condescension to threaten the foundations of the Republic. We must not look for "black men" or "white men," but for people of destructive intent who have taken their cue from the common devaluation of life and the expectations of human dignity we have so long encouraged by example and by default.

NO-FAULT RECONCILIATION

We Americans, whatever our color, need to rethink the principles and presuppositions which structure our conditional approach to living with each other. We must learn to accept each other with appreciation for what we are and for what we can become while daring to hope and to believe that we ourselves will be so accepted. It will not be easily accomplished. Too much "history" and too much that masquerades as history get in the way. But history, real or imagined, is always what is past and can only be justified in context. So must our own determinations be made in context, lest the incoherence in the history we leave compound the dilemma bequeathed by the history we received. Blacks know, for example, that not all the devils in the world are blue-eyed white males. It is time to say that. We do not enhance the principle of personal culpability by branding all those of a class of cohorts as ipso facto a class of culpables.

By the same logic, all of our social misfits are not young black studs hunting in packs and rapping out the frustrations their daddies brought back from 'Nam and the Persian Gulf in jungle rhythms punctuated with obscenities. In 'Nam and in the Gulf there was no black and white, just buddy-buddy. Brothers in arms; sometimes in the very arms of death. Back at home, it is a pale horse of a different color, but it is still death, and if you don't like it, you can at least rap about it. Somebody may get the message eventually.

The prevailing American tradition damns all blacks with the same tar brush and baptizes all whites in the same bucket of whitewash irrespective of merit or consent. Stifled in between these blankets of blame and blessing, an undetermined number of self-conscious individuals reject the dubious endowments of conventional wisdom in favor of being free to be themselves on their own terms. In the challenge ahead, we will need to identify these moral mavericks, for they will have prominent roles to play in the social greening of the world that is on its way. We sense that they are there, but we do not always know who they are. What we do know is that black people and white people alike range from degeneracy to heroism, but they are all people, mere people, substantially like ourselves.

This society will take a quantum leap forward when we learn to look for and to celebrate the many positives that spangle our long travail together. It is not disloyal to the cause, however that cause is defined, to recognize through all the murkiness of self-interest the uniqueness of the human endowment when it is performing at its best. The supreme disloyalty is not to a bell that has tolled itself into silence, but to the bell that has yet to ring. In our contemporary struggle for self-affirmation through the appreciation of others, we could, for example, remember with profit the patient, caring black women who over the countless generations of the Anglo-African odyssey nurtured and cared for the sons and daughters of white Americans, often to the neglect of their own. Surely these women were a national treasure, as were those selfless white women who forfeited fame, fortune, marriage, and leisure to plant the liberating torch of literacy and education in the stygian darkness so lately punctured by "emancipation." The Civil Rights movement was made up of inspired and intrepid coalitions of Blacks-and-whites-together, who ignored the fickle lines of race and gender and religion and marched through the gates of hell to redeem the soul of America. We have all that to build on, and that spirit, though bruised and muted, is not dead. We must not forfeit by default what cost so much to wring out of our own recalcitrance. There are white people and black people next door or across town who know that the future is here and are prepared to endorse it if they can hear a word of encouragement, or see a gesture of support. But there is still risk in ignoring convention, in being out of step with the agents of panic and the gurus of political correctness. It is time now to reach for the hand that is reaching for tomorrow, whatever color that hand may be. The evening of today is already far spent.

We must get on with the future of our country and our world. It will be a future in which the claims of race and place will be denied and rebuffed until they die for want of nurture, or it will be no future at all. The world has grown too small for bigotry, too tired for casuistry, and too uncertain for temporizing. People everywhere are in serious reevaluation of what it means to live, and what conditions of living are unacceptable for the human imprimatur wherever it may be found.

By any estimate, we have a lot going for us here in America. We live in the world's greatest democracy; we are the world's most advanced humanitarian society; our nation is the world's most renowned and effective citadel of freedom. We excel the rest of the world in technological proficiency and genius and creativity. We have unfathomable reservoirs of self-confidence and inexhaustible fountains of optimism.

We are all colors, all creeds, all nationalities. *We are Americans, the people of the dream.* Such is our self-perception. We can be more than that when we learn to use our singular advantages and achievements in the true humanizing of the social order, and in the creation of the truly responsible society. Americans have deep wellsprings of self-reliance, and we are not readily given to admissions of failure or self-doubt. Yet we know, if only because we are too American *not* to know, that we can be better than we are. We can excel in whatever we undertake with conviction.

The record speaks for itself! In science and technology. In medicine and communications. In the mapping of space and the production of energy, and so on ad infinitum the record speaks most eloquently. We have won enough Nobel Prizes to consider that achievement a national property. Yet the signs and the symbols of our dismal record in coming to terms with our humanity wink back at us with silent accusation like frozen stars in a firmament of moral expectation. We can be better than we are. Our failures fly in the face of an ethical commitment that is stated or implicit in all of the critical foundations of the culture: religion, law, and citizenship, and all the rest. In America the right to be human is the right to participate in all of the common ventures afforded by a just and humane society.

Now we must prepare for a new society which gives full honor to what we profess. We do not have much time, for the new order for which we must prepare is already here in prospect and expectation. We must not let the lingering haze of the smoldering fires of yesterday obscure the possibilities inherent in tomorrow. If we do not learn to trust each other, we cannot truly trust ourselves. The stresses of contemporary civilization are multifarious and multiplying. But one variable claims attention above all the rest. It seems that all over the world, in the words of Omar Khayyám: *men want dug up again,* which is to say that faceless and long-abused people are demanding and dying for recognition of the right to be human and to be so recognized—to have life with dignity, creativity, and responsibility. That, it seems to me, is neither unreasonable nor impossible. We all belong in the forefront of human enfranchisement. That is the least we can do for our country; that is the most we can do for each other; that is the best we can do for ourselves and for our posterity. That is the ultimate meaning of survival, and the only strategy that will work. I call it no-fault reconciliation—the recognition that we are all of a kind, with the same vulnerabilities, the same possibilities, and the same needs for God and each other.

About the Author. C. Eric Lincoln is William Rand Kenan, Jr. Professor Emeritus of Religion and Culture at Duke University. His widely acclaimed publications include *The Black Muslims in America; The Black Church since Frazier; Race, Religion, and the Continuing American Dilemma; The Black Experience in Religion;* and *The Black Church in the African American Experience* (with Lawrence H. Mamiya). He is the founding president of the Black Academy of Arts and Letters and a Fellow of the American Academy of Arts and Sciences. He has been awarded many honorary degrees and is listed in *Who's Who in America* and *Who's Who in the World.*

Library of Congress Cataloging-in-Publication Data
Lincoln, C. Eric (Charles Eric), 1924–
Coming through the fire : surviving race and place in America
C. Eric Lincoln.
ISBN 0-8223-1736-2 (cloth : alk. paper)
1. Racism—United States.   2. United States—Race relations.   3. Lincoln, C. Eric (Charles Eric), 1924–
—Biography.   4. Afro-American authors—20th century—Biography.
E185.615.L479   1996
305.8'00973—dc20   95-40107   CIP